Collyer's Library - Phone 01403 216548

XX32506

641.596

African
COOKING

THE COLLEGE OF
RICHARD COLLYER
LIBRARY

D1335870

African

COOKING

The best-kept secrets
from West to East

Ola Olaore

foulsham

LONDON • NEW YORK • TORONTO • SYDNEY

foulsham

The Oriel, Thames Valley Court, 183–187 Bath Road, Slough, Berkshire,
SL1 4AA, England
Foulsham books can be found in all good bookshops and direct from
www.foulsham.com
ISBN: 978-0-572-01131-4
Copyright © 1980 and 2008 Ola Olare
Cover photograph © Cephas Picture Library
A CIP record for this book is available from the British Library
The moral right of the author has been asserted
All rights reserved
The Copyright Act prohibits (subject to certain very limited exceptions) the
making of copies of any copyright work or of a substantial part of such work,
including the making of copies by photocopying or similar process. Written
permission to make a copy or copies must therefore normally be obtained from
the publisher in advance. It is advisable also to consult the publisher if in any
doubt as to the legality of any copying which is to be undertaken.

Printed in Great Britain by Printwise (Haverhill) Ltd, Haverhill

CONTENTS

INTRODUCTION

Africa's social life centres around food – good wholesome food. The sound of festive drums is all we need to bring out our cooking pots and pans and produce an array of exotic dishes. African cuisine is an experience and I have heard Afro-Americans describe it as 'soul food'.

Fortunately the African continent is blessed with some of the most fertile land on earth, yielding succulent fresh fruits, grain and vegetable crops in dazzling variety, yet unspoilt by modern agricultural chemical fads. The land is excellent for raising and producing meat animals and fowls which are among the tastiest in the world. Our seas and rivers contain some of the best fish.

The bulk in African diets is given by bananas, plantains (the large starchy banana used as a vegetable), yams, sweet potatoes, cassava and other tuberous roots, all starchy and full of carbohydrates. To ensure a balanced and nutritious diet we eat a lot of vegetables cooked in rich meat or fish sauces and a good deal of fresh fruit, which we have in abundance. Dozens of types of nuts and a variety of grain crops provide an excellent source of proteins.

A great many Europeans and Americans work in Africa. The question of how to use local ingredients is just as important to these expatriates as it is to adventurous European cooks, and a vast number of African housewives. Certainly European and American cooks are adventurous; they enjoy trying out foreign dishes. I have lost count of the number of recipes I have been cajoled into writing on the backs of cigarette packets or any piece of paper at hand. I have answered endless questions about 'those fat roots of yours'; 'those long green things'; 'sweet potatoes, yams, what do they taste like?'. Now it is down on paper. Of the hundreds of African dishes in every country, I have set down my favourite recipes, those which are easy to cook and for which ingredients are reasonably easy to obtain. Moreover, I have limited the regional specialities to avoid repetition since countries in the same geographical belts have the same crops and tend to do the same things with them. All the recipes, except where stated, are for six servings.

The usual African meal is just one course made up of any of the Main Meals. In the afternoons, however, a snack is served in most households but fruits are eaten at any time at all throughout the day. There is, of course, ample scope for the Europeans to combine the dishes into a meal of several courses, or for buffets.

The essential purpose of this book is **fun**; watch out for the pepper and have fun cooking and eating the African way.

Obtaining ingredients

Some African ingredients are available, even if sometimes at a price, in Europe and America. The West Indies have more or less the same ingredients naturally. So it is easy to obtain them and thereby enjoy African dishes anywhere in the world.

There are specialist foodstores which stock many African foods. In London, for instance, they are available at shops and open market stalls in Brixton, Dalston, Finsbury Park, Kilburn, Shepherds Bush and many Indian shops. Most large urban districts in Britain will have shops, in both the High Streets and the markets, which cater for shoppers from Africa, the Middle East and the Indian sub-continent. In other parts of Europe, and in America, African residents and students find they can obtain most of the ingredients needed to cook the national dishes. Some ingredients can be expensive, especially perishables which have to be flown over.

GLOSSARY

Amala is yam flour pudding

Anan geil is camel's milk

Berbere is an Ethiopian word for red pepper or chilli powder

Bitterleaf is a vegetable valued for its bitter-sweet taste, which needs much washing to prepare it for use

Brees is rice

Cassava is a plant (*Manihot utilissima*) introduced into Africa from South America at the beginning of the 17th century. It produces a number of thick fleshy tubers, full of starch which can be harvested throughout the year. It must be processed before use to rid it of poisonous juice. In Europe and America it is found as tapioca

Daddawa is the Hausa word for *iru*, a seasoning vegetable.

Dawa is a barley-type millet

Eba is cassava flour pudding

Efo is the Yoruba word for spinach of which there are some dozen types

Egusi is a seasoning made from the seeds of a cross between a gourd and a pumpkin. The seeds are like small almonds

Elubo is yam flour

Ewedu is a type of green vegetable

Gali, gari, garri are all terms for cassava flour

Garden egg is the name by which aubergine or eggplant is known in Africa

Gero, acha are specific millet varieties

Groundnuts are known in Europe and America as peanuts. Those used in these recipes are roasted without added oil, so do not substitute over-salted oil-fried cocktail nuts

Hillib is a Somali term for meat

Iru is a vegetable seasoning made from the beans of the African 'locust' tree, *Parkia biglandulosa* or *Parkia africana;* it should not be confused with the Mediterranean Carob or Locust tree, *Ceratonia siliqua,* which produces locust beans.

Jero is millet

Kaun is the Nigerian name for potash or rock salt, used for softening vegetables or dried beans. The nearest equivalent is bicarbonate of soda

Kimbo is butter or margarine

Kuka powder comes from the leaves of the baobab tree

Lalu powder is a seasoning made from the seeds of the baobab tree

Lansur is a parsley-like leaf vegetable

Malsouqua are very thin sheets of pastry made from semolina. The prepared '*phyllo*' pastry from Greek bakeries can be substituted

Matoke is the Ugandan word for plantain

Mealie is millet, a grain native to Africa

Mogo is the Ugandan word for cassava

Ogili is another name for iru

Okra or okro is an annual vegetable. The seed pods are gathered and cooked while green. Watch out. Because the pods are full of thick tasty juice, okra boils over very easily

Panla is stockfish – cod, saithe or ling, imported from Norway

Plantains are large bananas with green to reddish skins, used as a starchy vegetable

Ponkie is an African word for pumpkin

Sweet potatoes are tubers from a trailing plant, *Ipomoea batatas*. The flesh is yellow or orange and **has** a sweetish flavour

Steaming. Many African dishes are steamed, rather than simmered. If you do not have a double saucepan then simply place a trivet in the bottom of your saucepan.

Tabil is mixed ground spice

Tef is an Ethiopian grain

Tsamia, 'souring pods'

Tuwon chinkafa or Rice *tuwo* are names for Stiff Rice Pudding

Tuwon dawa is a stiff pudding made from millet flour

Wot, in Ethiopia, means sauce

Yams are large brown tubers produced by a vine, *Dioscorea rotundata*, which matures all year round. They can be stored by hanging in a dry place

Chapter One

STIFF PUDDINGS, *FUFUS* AND ACCOMPANIMENTS TO MAIN DISHES

The most characteristic dish in the African cuisine is a rich casserole, using a variety of meats or fish, which may be fresh, dried or smoked. The casserole is seasoned with exotic spices native to the continent and varies in texture between a thick soup and a stew. It is always served with a starchy dish made from various grains, and roots. For example, white rice with stew is eaten by one in four Africans at least once a week. It is everybody's Sunday special and can be equated with the European or American roasted joint of meat in importance. Although all it consists of is boiled white rice and a dish like Sunday Stew, no African cookery book is complete without it.

Sometimes the casserole is enhanced further by the addition of a sauce, like Pepper Sauce or *Ewedu* Sauce, and these are included in this chapter.

Fufu is the collective name by which certain stiff puddings are called, whether they are made from flour derived from corn (maize) or cassava, or whether the pudding is made of boiled and pounded yam. These puddings or dough-like dishes are the main ingredient of the meal but cannot be eaten on their own. They are always the partners of the soups or stews.

WHITE RICE

INGREDIENTS

	Imperial	Metric	American
brown rice	*1 lb*	*450 g*	*2 cups*
salt to taste			

Wash rice well, drain. Boil 2 pints/1 litre/5 cups of water in a cooking pot and add the rice. Reduce heat and boil rice for about 20 minutes, drain and rinse rice 2 or 3 times to reduce excess starch. Put back on the fire with salt to taste and a cup of water. Cook until rice is cooked all the moisture absorbed. Serve rice hot with rich meat stew, like Sunday Stew (page 25).

EBA (CASSAVA
(CASSAVA GRAIN PUDDING)

Nigeria

Stir 8 oz/225 g/2 cups of *garri* (cassava grains) into a bowl of boiling water. Drain off excess water and allow garri to settle and absorb moisture. Stir until stiff and smooth. Serve with any soup and/or stew.

RICE TUWO
(STIFF RICE PUDDING)

Stir 1 lb/450 g/8½ cups of cooked unsalted rice with a wooden spoon until almost smooth. Mould and put in a dish. Serve with *taushe* soup (page 00), and browned butter or with bean soup, *gbegiri* (page 20).

There are many other types of main dish with which soups and stews are eaten like the corn *fufu*, cassava flour *fufu*, cassava paste *fufu*, *amala* (yam flour *fufu*), etc. They are mainly starchy carbohydrates. Served with protein, mineral and vitamin-rich soups and stews, they provide a filling, balanced diet. The various millet (*gero*, *dawa*, *acha*) puddings are, however, rich with their own proteins.

FLOUR-BASED FUFU
(FOR TWO)

INGREDIENTS	Imperial	Metric	American
Water	1 pint	500 ml	2½ cups
Flour (Yam or Cassava)	1 lb	450 g	3 cups

Bring water to the boil in a cooking pot. With a wooden spoon or spatula, stir some of the flour into the water and blend until smooth. Reduce the heat at this point to avoid lumps forming. Blend in the rest of the flour until the pudding is stiff but soft and smooth. Serve with meat or fish stew and/or vegetable soup.

INE-OKA

Nigeria

INGREDIENTS	Imperial	Metric	American
Maize flour (cornmeal)	*1 lb*	*450 g*	*3 cups*
Water	*1 pint*	*500 ml*	*2½ cups*

Boil water in a saucepan. Reduce the heat and stir in a little maize flour; keep stirring while the pudding cooks. Stir in more flour until pudding is stiff but soft. Mix well until it is quite smooth. Turn into a dish and serve hot with *agbono* soup (page 53).

POUNDED YAM FUFU

Nigeria

INGREDIENTS	Imperial	Metric	American
Yam	*6 lbs*	*2.7 kg*	*6 lb*

Peel, slice and wash *yam*. Boil with 2 pints/1.10 litres/5 cups of water (no salt). When *yam* is cooked, strain out of the water into a mortar and pound well with a pestle adding a little hot water to soften the texture. Pound until *fufu* is satiny smooth, mould and put into a serving dish. Serve hot with meat or fish stew and vegetable or okra soup.

SWEET POTATO AND YAM FUFU

Nigeria

INGREDIENTS	Imperial	Metric	American
Sweet potatoes	*2 lb*	*1 kg*	*2 lb*
Yams	*2 lb*	*1 kg*	*2 lb*
Water to cook			

First prepare the *yams*, by peeling, and place them in a cooking pot, just covering them with water. Boil them until they begin to soften, then add the peeled sweet potatoes and continue boiling until they are both cooked. Lift the *yams* and sweet potatoes from the water into a mortar and pound with a pestle until they are satiny smooth and like a soft dough in texture, adding a very small quantity of boiling water to soften if required. Mould the mixture into shape in a serving dish, and eat with fish or meat stew or vegetable soup.

PLANTAIN AND YAM FUFU

 Ghana

INGREDIENTS	Imperial	Metric	American
Plantains	2 lb	1 kg	2 lb
Yams	2 lb	1 kg	2 lb
Water			

Peel the *yams* and cook in enough water to cover. When they are nearly done, add the peeled plantains and cook together until both are soft. Drain them and place in a mortar; pound with a pestle until they are satiny smooth. Add up to 4 fl. oz/100 ml/½ cup of boiling water, if necessary, to soften the pudding which should be the texture of soft dough. Place in a dish and shape it neatly. Serve with meat stews, fish dishes or soup.

APU

 Nigeria

INGREDIENTS	Imperial	Metric	American
Yam	2 lb	1 kg	2 lb
Plantain	2	2	2
Garri *pudding*	8 oz	225 g	½ lb

Peel the *yam* and plantain. Rinse, cut into chunks, cover with water and cook without salt in a saucepan until soft and done. Lift *yam* and plantain out of saucepan into a mortar and with a pestle crush and pound them until mixture is satiny smooth. Add the *garri* pudding and continue to pound until mixture is thoroughly blended. If too stiff, add a little hot water and blend it into the *apu*. Mould *apu* into a smooth shape and place in a vegetable dish. Serve hot with *agbono* soup (page 53) or any vegetable soup.

AMALA
(YAM FLOUR PUDDING)

 Nigeria

INGREDIENTS	Imperial	Metric	American
Elubo *(yam flour)*	8 oz	225 g	½ lb
Water	1 pint	500 ml	2½ cups

Bring the water to the boil in a saucepan, lower the heat and stir one-third of the flour in with a spatula or wooden spoon. Then stir in the rest of the flour and blend well into a stiff but soft pudding. Turn into a dish and serve hot with bean soup (page 20).

EKURU

Nigeria

INGREDIENTS

	Imperial	Metric	American
Black-eyed beans, skinned	½ lb	225 g	½ lb
Salt to taste			
Leaves or aluminium foil to wrap			

To skin beans: soak for 30 minutes, drain off water and, with a squeezing washing action with both hands, peel the skin off the beans. Cover with water and the skins will float. Collect the skins in a sieve as you drain the water off into a second bowl. Skin the odd beans left and repeat action. As the skin is the nutritious part of the beans, it is not absolutely necessary to skin them, but the black bits of the 'eyes' make the mixture look unattractive.

Soak skinned black-eyed beans until soft. Grind or liquidize, pour into a mixing bowl and beat well, adding salt. Shape leaves or foil sheets 7 in. by 7 in./17.5 cm by 17.5 cm and put four tablespoons of bean purée in each. Arrange on a steamer in a saucepan with a pint of water. Cover pot and steam *ekuru* for 45 minutes. When it is cooked, a fork stuck into it should come out clean. Take *ekuru* out of the leaves or foil, allow to cool slightly, mash to loosen the pudding and mix with pepper sauce (page 26). Serve hot.

IRIO

Kenya

INGREDIENTS

	Imperial	Metric	American
Maize (sweet corn)	2 lb	1 kg	4 cups
Kidney beans or peas	1 lb	450 g	2 cups
Potatoes	2 lb	1 kg	2 lb
Green cooking bananas	4	4	4
Kimbo *(margarine)*	2 tbsp	2 tbsp	2 tbsp
Salt to taste			

Boil the corn in a deep saucepan with a pint of water until it is soft. Peel and wash the bananas and potatoes and add them to the corn. Add the beans or peas, cover pot and reduce the heat. Continue to simmer until food is cooked and all the water has been absorbed. Stir in the margarine and salt and simmer for a further 15 minutes. Mash all the cooked ingredients together and serve with meat gravy (page 45).

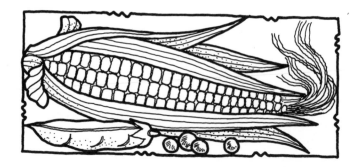

MATOKE

 Uganda

INGREDIENTS	Imperial	Metric	American
Large green plantains	4	4	4
or small green cooking bananas	6	6	6
Washed banana leaves or foil to wrap	4	4	4
Salt to taste			
Butter to taste			

Peel plantains and wrap in banana leaves or foil. Arrange in a deep saucepan with a pint of water and poach for about an hour. Turn plantains out into a bowl and mash well, adding butter. Serve with chicken or meat sauce.

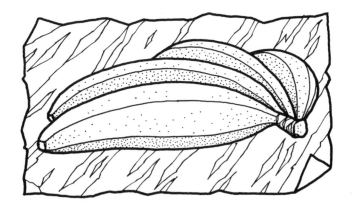

EGBO

 Nigeria

INGREDIENTS	Imperial	Metric	American
Polished maize (cornmeal)	1 lb	450 g	1 lb
Pepper Sauce			
Palm nut oil	4 fl. oz	100 ml	½ cup
Chilli powder	1 tsp	1 tsp	1 tsp
Fresh peppers, ground	4	4	4
Large tomatoes, ground	2	2	2
Medium onion, ground	1	1	1
Salt to taste			
Spring onions (onion leaf), chopped	2	2	2

Pour the maize into a bowl and soak overnight. Drain and rinse, then pour into a saucepan and cook with 1 pint/500 ml/2½ cups of water until it is soft. Add more water if necessary.

When the maize is cooked, stir with a wooden spoon, mashing as you stir. Serve hot with the pepper sauce.

Pepper Sauce

Meanwhile heat the oil for 10 minutes. Reduce the heat and allow to cool slightly. Add the rest of the ingredients to the hot oil and, stirring constantly, fry the condiments to make a tasty sauce. Add the chopped onion leaves, and simmer for 10 minutes.

UGALI

Kenya

INGREDIENTS

	Imperial	Metric	American
Maize flour (cornmeal)	*1 lb*	*450 g*	*3 cups*
Boiling water	*1 pint*	*560 ml*	*2½ cups*

Boil the water in a saucepan and, with a wooden spoon or spatula, stir in sufficient maize flour to make a thick, stiff pudding. Stir well to achieve a smooth satiny finish. Turn into a vegetable dish. Serve with Vegetable Soup.

Vegetable Soup	Imperial	Metric	American
Margarine	*3 tbsp*	*3 tbsp*	*3 tbsp*
Beef, cubed	*2 lb*	*1 kg*	*2 lb*
Medium onion, chopped	*1*	*1*	*1*
Cabbage, finely shredded	*1 lb*	*450 g*	*1 lb*
Maize flour	*2 tbsp*	*2 tbsp*	*2 tbsp*
Large ripe tomatoes, chopped	*2*	*2*	*2*
Lemon juice	*½ tsp*	*½ tsp*	*½ tsp*
Chilli powder	*½ tsp*	*½ tsp*	*½ tsp*
Salt to taste			

Melt the margarine in a saucepan. Wash the meat and pat dry, then fry in the melted fat until light brown. Add the onion and continue to fry. Add the lemon juice and salt. Add the chilli powder and tomatoes, stirring constantly. Wash and drain the cabbage, add to the soup with ½ pint/250 ml/1¼ cups of water. Cover pot and simmer for 20 minutes. Serve hot with *ugali*.

EWEDU SAUCE

Nigeria

INGREDIENTS

	Imperial	Metric	American
Ewedu leaves	*1 lb*	*450 g*	*1 lb*
Chilli powder or ground fresh peppers	*½ tsp*	*½ tsp*	*½ tsp*
Iru (daddawa)	*2 tsp*	*2 tsp*	*2 tsp*
Ground crayfish	*1 tsp*	*1 tsp*	*1 tsp*
or *cube chicken stock*	*1*	*1*	*1*
Salt to taste			

Put 2 cups of water, chilli powder and *iru* in a cooking pot and cook for 30 minutes. Meanwhile rinse *ewedu* leaves and finely shred with a sharp knife on a chopping board. Add to the seasoned boiling water and simmer for 5—10 minutes. Turn the heat off. Stir in the crayfish and salt; or crush in the chicken stock cube. Serve warm with *fufu* (page 13), *apu* (page 15), or *eba* (page 12) as a sauce in addition to a rich meat or fish stew.

Chapter Two

SOUPS AND STEWS

TAUSHE

INGREDIENTS	Imperial	Metric	American
Brisket of beef or breast of lamb	2 lb	1 kg	2 lb
Large tomatoes, chopped	2	2	2
Large onion, chopped	1	1	1
Raw groundnuts, skinned and ground	4 oz	100 g	¼ lb
Pepper, ground	½ tbsp	½ tbsp	½ tbsp
Pumpkin, diced	6 oz	150 g	1¼ cups
Spring onions, diced	4	4	4
Green leaf vegetable	8 oz	225 g	½ lb
Cooking oil or groundnut oil	4 tbsp	4 tbsp	4 tbsp
Salt to taste			

Chop brisket or lamb breast and combine meat, tomatoes, salt, onion, pepper, spring onion and cooking oil in a saucepan with 16 fl. oz/400 ml/2 cups of water. Cook for 30 minutes. Add the pumpkin and cook for a further 20 minutes. Add the groundnuts and chopped green leaves, reduce the heat and cook for 20 minutes. Serve with stiff rice pudding (*tuwon chinkafa*) (page 13), or millet flour pudding (*tuwon dawa*), sprinkled with fried, salted butter.

EFO

INGREDIENTS	Imperial	Metric	American
Efo (green leaf vegetable), parboiled	1 lb	450 g	1 lb
Fresh tomatoes, ground or liquidized	1 lb	450 g	1 lb
Meat (beef, mutton or pork)	1 lb	450 g	1 lb
Smoked fish	1 lb	450 g	1 lb
Large onion, ground or liquidized	1	1	1
Crayfish, ground	1 tbsp	1 tbsp	1 tbsp
Hard-boiled eggs	4	4	4
Pepper, ground	½ tbsp	½ tbsp	½ tbsp
Salt to taste			

Boil the meat with the salt and a small amount of onion, until tender. Heat the oil and fry the meat. Take meat out when brown and put aside in a dish. To the hot oil, add the tomatoes, the rest of the onion, pepper, salt and crayfish, and cook for 30 minutes stirring constantly. Add the meat and eggs. Wash and bone the fish and add it with the green vegetable. Simmer for 10 minutes. Serve with eba (page 12), yam fufu (page 14), or rice.

There are no less than a dozen types of efo (spinach). Efo is the Yoruba name for green leaf vegetables in general.

GBEGIRI (BEAN SOUP)
(BEAN SOUP)

INGREDIENTS	Imperial	Metric	American
Black-eyed beans, skinned	4 oz	100 g	¼ lb
Pepper	1 tsp	1 tsp	1 tsp
Small onion	1	1	1
Dry smoked fish	1 lb	450 g	1 lb
Tomato purée	1 tbsp	1 tbsp	1 tbsp
Palmnut oil	6 tbsp	6 tbsp	6 tbsp
Mashed iru,	1 tsp	1 tsp	1 tsp
or Cube chicken stock	1	1	1

To skin beans: Soak for 30 minutes and then drain off the water. Using both hands with a squeezing, washing action, peel the skins off the beans. Cover with water and the skins will float and can be collected in a sieve or strainer as the water is drained off into a second bowl. Repeat the sequence to skin the remaining beans.

Boil the skinned beans for 45 minutes until very soft. Add the rest of the ingredients, except the fish, and cook for 30 minutes. Wash and bone the fish and add to the soup. Simmer for a further 15 minutes. Serve hot with amala (yam flour pudding, page 15), or rice tuwo (stiff rice pudding, page 13).

OKRA SOUP
(AS A SAUCE, TRADITONAL METHOD)

INGREDIENTS	Imperial	Metric	American
Okra, finely chopped	½ lb	225 g	½ lb
Mashed iru	1 tsp	1 tsp	1 tsp
or Cube chicken stock	1	1	1
Small piece of kaun	1	1	1
Water	16 fl. oz	400 ml	2 cups
Pepper	½ tsp	½ tsp	½ tsp
Ground crayfish	1 tsp	1 tsp	1 tsp
Salt to taste			

Combine the water, *iru* and pepper in a saucepan and cook for 15 minutes. Add the okra and *kaun* and cook for a further five minutes. Stir in the crayfish and the salt and remove soup from heat. Serve as sauce with fish or meat stew. Always watch okra all the time as it is likely to boil over, like milk, when your back is turned.

Iru is a vegetable seasoning made from the seeds of the fruits of the locust tree (Parkia biglandulosa). Kaun is a potash or rock-salt, used in softening vegetables or dry beans.

OKRA SOUP
(AS A SAUCE, EXPRESS METHOD)

INGREDIENTS	Imperial	Metric	American
Okra, finely chopped	8 oz	225 g	½ lb
Cube chicken stock	1	1	1
Water	12 fl. oz	300 ml	1½ cups
Salt			

Combine okra and water in a saucepan and cook for eight minutes, being careful not to let okra boil over. Crush in the chicken stock and a pinch of salt. Serve with fish or meat stew and eat with pounded *yam fufu* (page 14), or *eba* (cassava flour pudding, page 12).

OKRA SOUP PROPER

INGREDIENTS	Imperial	Metric	American
Okra, finely chopped	1 lb	450 g	1 lb
Meat (mutton, pork, beef or poultry)	1 lb	450 g	1 lb
Dry smoked fish	½ lb	225 g	½ lb
Ground crayfish	1 tsp	1 tsp	1 tsp
Ripe tomatoes	2	2	2
Tomato purée	½ tbsp	½ tbsp	½ tbsp
Small onion, sliced	½	½	½
Groundnut or palmnut oil	6 tbsp	6 tbsp	6 tbsp
Cube chicken stock	1	1	1
Pepper	1 tsp	1 tsp	1 tsp
Salt to taste			

Cook meat with salt and one slice of onion for 30 minutes. Grind or liquidize the tomatoes and onion, add to the meat with the chicken stock cube, tomato purée, pepper, cooking oil and two cups of water. Cook for 20 minutes. Wash and bone the dry fish, rinse well and add to the soup. Add the okra and simmer for 10—15 minutes. Stir in the ground crayfish. Turn off heat. Serve soup with pounded *yam fufu* (page 14), or fluffy white rice.

BOKOTO
(COWHEEL SOUP)

INGREDIENTS	Imperial	Metric	American
Cowheel, scraped clean and parboiled	½	½	½
Mixed spice	½ tbsp	½ tbsp	½ tbsp
Tomato purée	1 tbsp	1 tbsp	1 tbsp
Pepper, ground	½ tbsp	½ tbsp	½ tbsp
Cooking oil	4 tbsp	4 tbsp	4 tbsp
Large tomatoes, ground or liquidized	2	2	2
Onion, ground or liquidized	1	1	1
Salt to taste			

If you buy raw, ready-scraped cowheel, have the butcher chop it. Wash cowheel pieces, and put in a large saucepan with salt. Cover with water and boil for one hour until tender. Drain off water and rinse. Combine the cowheel and all the other ingredients in a clean saucepan and cook for 40 minutes. Serve with other soups and rice or *fufu* (page 13).

Usually cowheel is combined with other meats to make soups.

BITTERLEAF SOUP

INGREDIENTS	Imperial	Metric	American
Panla *(stockfish)*	*1 lb*	*450 g*	*1 lb*
Bitterleaf	*1 lb*	*450 g*	*1 lb*
Assorted meats	*1 lb*	*450 g*	*1 lb*
Smoked dry fish	*1 lb*	*450 g*	*1 lb*
Assorted offals	*1 lb*	*450 g*	*1 lb*
Cowheel, half-cooked	*1 lb*	*450 g*	*1 lb*
Land crabs, cooked	*1 lb*	*450 g*	*1 lb*
Egusi, *ground*	*8 oz*	*225 g*	*1 cup*
Tomato purée	*1 tbsp*	*1 tbsp*	*1 tbsp*
Iru (daddawa)	*1 tsp*	*1 tsp*	*1 tsp*
or *Cube chicken stock*	*1*	*1*	*1*
Ground crayfish	*2 tsp*	*2 tsp*	*2 tsp*
Large ripe tomatoes, ground or liquidized	*3*	*3*	*3*
Large onion, ground or liquidized	*1*	*1*	*1*
Palmnut oil or any cooking oil	*8 fl. oz*	*200 ml*	*1 cup*
Pepper or chilli powder	*2 tsp*	*2 tsp*	*2 tsp*

Soak *panla* overnight in salt water (using only one teaspoon salt). Wash *panla* well and cut into pieces. Cut the meats and offal and clean well. Combine meats, offal, cowheel, stockfish, salt, crabs and a cup of water in a large saucepan and cook for 20 minutes. Add the oil, the ground ingredients (except crayfish) and cook for 20 minutes.

Meanwhile wash the bitterleaf (a hard job – like washing cloth between the knuckles) until 90 per cent of the bitter taste is washed off. Rinse several times. Add the *egusi* to the soup, cook for 15 minutes and then add the bitterleaf. Stir in the crayfish and the washed and boned dry fish. Reduce heat and simmer for 15 minutes more. Serve hot with pounded *yam fufu* (page 14) or *eba* (page 12).

You need not serve all the soup at once as it will keep for several days if you re-heat it daily.

Panla is the stockfish of cod, saithe or white ling imported from Norway. Bitterleaf is hard work to wash, but the faint bitter-sweet taste left when it is cooked is well worth the effort. It foams when being washed, so rinse between washing. It is better prepared the day before. *Egusi* is the seed of melon, rather like small almonds.

ISIEWU

INGREDIENTS	Imperial	Metric	American
Goat, head and legs only	1	1	1
Chilli powder	½ tbsp	½ tbsp	½ tbsp
Lemon juice	1 tbsp	1 tbsp	1 tbsp
Tomato purée	1 tbsp	1 tbsp	1 tbsp
Mixed spice	1 tbsp	1 tbsp	1 tbsp
Cooking oil	4 tbsp	4 tbsp	4 tbsp
Large tomatoes, ground or liquidized	3	3	3
Medium onion, ground or liquidized	1	1	1
Small onion, sliced	1	1	1
Salt to taste			

On a barbecue-like open fire, singe the hairs off the head and legs of the goat without burning the skin. Scrape and singe alternatively until all the hairs are off. Burn the hoofs and horns and peel them off with the point of a heavy knife. Wash the head and legs thoroughly with soap and a rough sponge or brush. Chop up into small pieces and rinse well, discarding the brains. Pour the lemon juice on it and mix well. Leave aside for 10 minutes.

Combine meat, salt, sliced onion and spice in a saucepan and cook for 40 minutes. Add the pepper, tomatoes, onion and cooking oil and simmer for 40 minutes. Serve hot on its own.

Sheep can be used if preferred, for this superb Ibo soup.

Stuffed Peppers—page 30
with Dodo—page 84

SUNDAY STEW

INGREDIENTS	Imperial	Metric	American
Meat (beef, mutton or pork)	2 lb	1 kg	2 lb
Ripe tomatoes, ground or liquidized	1 lb	450 g	1 lb
Large onion, ground or liquidized	1	1	1
Tomatoes, sliced	2	2	2
Small onion, sliced	1	1	1
Tomato purée	2 tbsp	2 tbsp	2 tbsp
Chilli powder	½ tbsp	½ tbsp	½ tbsp
Groundnut oil	8 fl. oz	200 ml	1 cup
Pinch of thyme			
Salt to taste			

Cook the meat until tender with salt, thyme and two slices of onion, adding sufficient water to prevent burning. Heat oil in a saucepan and fry the drained meat until brown. Take out the meat and leave on one side in a pan. Put the sliced tomatoes and sliced onion in the hot oil in the saucepan and fry lightly. Add the rest of the ingredients, salt to taste and cook for 25 minutes, stirring constantly. Add the fried meat and simmer for 15 minutes more.

Fish can be used instead of meat. In this case, only steam the fish for 15 minutes to extract excess liquid before frying.

PEPPER SAUCE WITH LIVER

INGREDIENTS	Imperial	Metric	American
Liver	1 lb	450 g	1 lb
Ripe tomatoes, skinned	3	3	3
Onion	1	1	1
Groundnut oil	6 tbsp	6 tbsp	6 tbsp
Chilli powder	1 tsp	1 tsp	1 tsp
Dash of thyme and powdered coriander			
Salt to taste			

Cut liver into small pieces and boil with a pinch of salt and a cup of water for 20 minutes. Liquidize the tomatoes with half the onion, and slice the other half of onion. Heat oil, drain liver and fry lightly. Put the liver on one side in a pan. Lightly fry the sliced onion. Combine the rest of the ingredients with the liquidized mixture and stir into the hot oil. Cook for 25 minutes stirring constantly to prevent sticking. Add the fried liver and simmer for 5 minutes more. Serve hot with freshly baked bread, *yam*, sweet potatoes and cooked beans.

Chachanga—page 66

YOYO (SPRATS) PEPPER SAUCE

INGREDIENTS	Imperial	Metric	American
Yoyo	1 lb	450 g	1 lb
Mixed spice	½ tbsp	½ tbsp	½ tbsp
Salt to taste			
Pepper Sauce			
Tomatoes	3	3	3
Onion	1	1	1
Groundnut oil	6 tbsp	6 tbsp	6 tbsp
Chilli powder	1 tsp	1 tsp	1 tsp
Dash of thyme and coriander powder			
Salt to taste			

To make Pepper Sauce: liquidize the tomatoes with half the onion and slice the other half. Heat the oil, lightly fry the onion slices and combine the spices with the tomato mixture before stirring into the hot oil. Cook for 25 minutes, stirring constantly.

Cut and clean *yoyo*, drain and season with mixed spice and salt. Heat oil until quite hot and fry *yoyo* until cooked and crisp. Add *yoyo* to the Pepper Sauce.

Fried *yoyo* is sometimes eaten as a snack on its own, washed down with chilled beer.

ALAPA

INGREDIENTS	Imperial	Metric	American
Fresh fish	2 lb	1 kg	2 lb
Lime juice	1 tbsp	1 tbsp	1 tbsp
Large, ripe tomatoes	2	2	2
Medium onion	1	1	1
Tomato purée	½ tbsp	½ tbsp	½ tbsp
Cooking oil	4 tbsp	4 tbsp	4 tbsp
Chilli powder	1 tsp	1 tsp	1 tsp
Pinch of ground cloves			
Salt to taste			

Clean and wash the fish, salt it and squeeze the lime juice over it. Leave on one side for 20 minutes. Grind or liquidize the fresh tomatoes and onion. Combine all ingredients except the fish in a saucepan. Add two cups of water and simmer for 30 minutes. Add the fish and cook for a further 20 minutes. Serve hot with boiled *yam*, *cassava* or *fufu* (page 13).

Chapter Three

MEAT AND POULTRY

PORK PINEAPPLE

INGREDIENTS	Imperial	Metric	American
Pork or ham steak, cubed	2 lb	1 kg	2 lb
Small pineapple, peeled and diced	1	1	1
Cayenne pepper	1 tsp	1 tsp	1 tsp
Mixed spice	1 tsp	1 tsp	1 tsp

Cook cubed ham or pork with salt, two slices of onion and a cup of water. Lightly fry the meat, put in a pan and sprinkle with the cayenne and spice, thread pork or ham cube and pineapple cube onto cocktail sticks alternately.

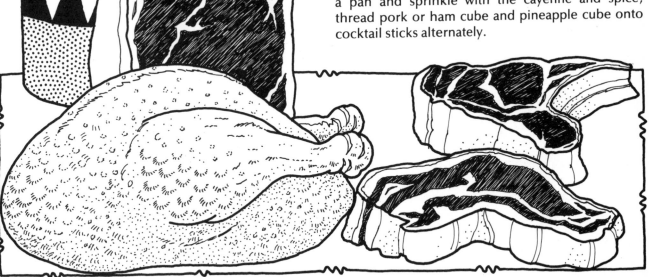

CHOPONE-CHOPTWO

INGREDIENTS	Imperial	Metric	American
Small onion, chopped	1	1	1
Mutton or beef, cooked	2 lb	1 kg	2 lb
Small green sweet pepper, thinly sliced	1	1	1
Small red sweet pepper, thinly sliced	1	1	1
Mixed spice	1 tsp	1 tsp	1 tsp
Flour, self-raising	4 oz	100 g	1 cup
or flour sifted with 1 tsp baking powder			
Knob of butter	4 oz	4 oz	4 oz
Eggs, beaten	2	2	2
Warm milky water	2 tbsp	2 tbsp	2 tbsp

Shred meat and mix with the spice, peppers, onion and salt. Work butter into sifted flour and baking powder until resembles breadcrumbs. Whisk one beaten egg into the warm water and stir a little at a time into the flour to make a soft but firm dough. Roll out on a floured board and cut into rectangles 6 in. by 4 in./15 cm by 10 cm. Put one tablespoon of meat mixture on each pastry rectangle and seal together the two short ends, leaving two open ends (like sausage rolls). Arrange on a greased baking sheet and bake in the centre of a pre-heated oven for 30—40 minutes at 350 °F/180 °C/Gas Mark 4.

You can also fry them in shallow oil. Serve hot with vegetables.

CURRIED MEAT TRIANGLES

INGREDIENTS	Imperial	Metric	American
Beef or mutton, cooked and minced	2 lb	1 kg	2 lb
Curry powder	1 tbsp	1 tbsp	1 tbsp
Small onion, chopped	1	1	1
Shortcrust pastry	8 oz	225 g	½ lb
Oil to fry			
Salt to taste			

Mix minced, cooked meat with curry powder, onion and salt. Roll out pastry and cut into squares 4 in. by 4 in./10 cm by 10 cm. Put a tablespoon of meat mixture on each pastry square. Brush edges of squares with milk and fold over to form triangles. Seal edges with a fork. Fry each side of meat triangles until golden brown. Serve hot with vegetables.

GUINEA-FOWL WITH ORANGE

INGREDIENTS	Imperial	Metric	American
Guinea-fowl	1	1	1
Oranges, squeezed for the juice	2	2	2
Oranges peeled and sliced thinly	3	3	3
Cube chicken stock	1	1	1
Lime or lemon juice	1 tsp	1 tsp	1 tsp
Honey	1 tsp	1 tsp	1 tsp
Cider or wine	1 tbsp	1 tbsp	1 tbsp
White pepper	1 tsp	1 tsp	1 tsp
Mixed spice	1 tsp	1 tsp	1 tsp
Flour	1 tsp	1 tsp	1 tsp
Salt to taste			

Clean the guinea-fowl, carefully extracting the giblets. Wash well and rub the inside with lime juice. Place in a deep saucepan, crumble in the chicken cube and add ½ pint/250 ml/1¼ cups of water and the rest of the ingredients, except the sliced oranges. Cover pot and steam over a low heat for about one hour. Take the fowl out of the stock and put it in a roasting tin. Pour on it a little melted butter and brown it in a hot oven for 30 minutes. Serve on a platter and arrange orange slices around it.

PEPPER CHICKEN

INGREDIENTS	Imperial	Metric	American
Chicken breasts or pullets	6	6	6
Large onion, sliced	1	1	1
Large ripe tomatoes, sliced	2	2	2
Tomato purée	1 tbsp	1 tbsp	1 tbsp
Chilli powder	1 tsp	1 tsp	1 tsp
Cooking oil	4 fl. oz	100 ml	½ cup
Mixed spice	1 tsp	1 tsp	1 tsp
Butter	1 tsp	1 tsp	1 tsp

Clean and wash the chicken. Place in a sauce-pan with salt, some onion, half a pint of water and a dash of thyme. Cover pot and simmer for 45 minutes. Take out chicken and place in a baking tin, sprinkle with melted butter and brown in pre-heated oven for 30 minutes. Meanwhile, heat the oil in a saucepan and lightly fry the onion, add the rest of the ingredients and fry gently over a low heat. Add two tablespoons of stock from the boiled chicken and continue to fry until the moisture has evaporated. Arrange chicken on a platter, pour the pepper sauce over it and serve accompanied by a plate of fluffy white rice.

STUFFED VEGETABLES

INGREDIENTS	Imperial	Metric	American
Medium onions	6	6	6
Roundish green sweet peppers	6	6	6
Medium firm ripe tomatoes	6	6	6
Corned beef (minced)	2 lb	1 kg	2 lb
Breast of pork, diced	1 lb	450 g	1 lb
Onion, chopped	1	1	1
Tomato, diced	1	1	1
Cooked rice	4 tbsp	4 tbsp	4 tbsp
Butter	1 oz	25 g	⅛ cup
Breadcrumbs	2 oz	50 g	½ cup
Mixed spice	2 tsp	2 tsp	2 tsp
White pepper	1 tsp	1 tsp	1 tsp
Salt to taste			

Peel the onions and scoop out the insides. Cut 'lids' off the peppers and tomatoes at the stalk ends, and scoop out the insides. Discard the pepper seeds but chop or mince the flesh scooped out of the onions and tomatoes and add to the rest of the ingredients. Boil the pork, allow to cool and mince. Melt the butter and fry the onions, add the corned beef and minced pork and fry for 10 minutes. Add the spice, pepper, salt and rice and let it all heat through thoroughly. Fill the onion, tomato and pepper cases with the mixture and top each with breadcrumbs. Arrange stuffed vegetables on a roasting tray and bake for 10 minutes in pre-heated oven.

DRUMSTICKS

INGREDIENTS	Imperial	Metric	American
Chicken drumsticks **or** guinea-fowl **or** turkey	6	6	6
Roasted groundnuts, ground	3 tbsp	3 tbsp	3 tbsp
Chilli powder	1 tsp	1 tsp	1 tsp
Mixed spice	2 tsp	2 tsp	2 tsp
Salt to taste			
Oil to deep fry			

Wash and dry drumsticks. Mix together the dry ingredients and spread on a flat surface or board. Roll each drumstick in the groundnut mixture, coating it well. Leave for 20 minutes for the coating to settle. Deep fry in hot oil, and serve hot. Alternatively you may put the drumsticks in foil and bake in an oven until cooked. Remove foil and grill or place under broiler for a further 10 minutes to brown.

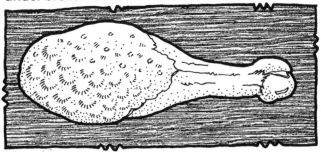

TINKO

INGREDIENTS	Imperial	Metric	American
Combination of liver, heart, kidney, meat, snails	3 lb	1.35 kg	3 lb
Lime, fresh	1	1	1
Chilli powder	2 tsp	2 tsp	2 tsp
Onion	1	1	1
Salt			
Oil to deep fry			

Shell snails and rub with salt and lime. Wash well until they are no longer slimy, slice in half lengthwise and wash thoroughly again. Cut the other meats and offal into pieces and wash well. Boil all together in a saucepan with salt, onion and a cup of water. Cook until meat is tender and well cooked. Heat oil and deep fry for about 20 minutes so that *tinko* is fairly dry and crisp. Sprinkle with chilli powder and serve hot or cold with chilled beer. The snails used in this recipe are the African 'bush' snails, available in some 'Continental' foodstores or market stalls specialising in African and Asian foodstuffs. The offal can be beef, mutton or goat meat.

KIDNEY RICE BALLS

INGREDIENTS	Imperial	Metric	American
Ox kidney, cooked and minced	2 lb	1 kg	2 lb
Cooked rice	6 tbsp	6 tbsp	6 tbsp
Eggs, beaten	2	2	2
Small onion, chopped	1	1	1
Mixed spice	1 tsp	1 tsp	1 tsp
Cornflakes, crushed	1 oz	25 g	1 cup
Salt to taste			

Mix together the kidney, rice, onion and spice, mould into balls and lower into the egg. Roll them in the cornflakes and deep fry in hot oil. Serve hot garnished with fresh tomatoes and lettuce. Liver can be used instead of kidneys. A few slices of lightly fried liver or kidney, served with the rice balls will turn this lovely dish into a full meal.

PIGEONS ON SALAD

INGREDIENTS	Imperial	Metric	American
Good-sized pigeons	6	6	6
Mixed spice	2 tsp	2 tsp	2 tsp
Salt			
Oil to deep fry			

Clean pigeons and remove giblets. Wash well and rub inside with salt and spice. Leave for 20 minutes. Heat oil and deep fry pigeons. Alternatively, you can wrap pigeons in foil and roast in pre-heated oven for about 40 minutes. Remove foil to allow pigeons to brown for 15 minutes. Serve on a bed of crisp salad on a platter.

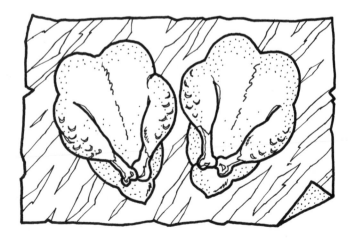

Chapter Four

REGIONAL SPECIALITIES

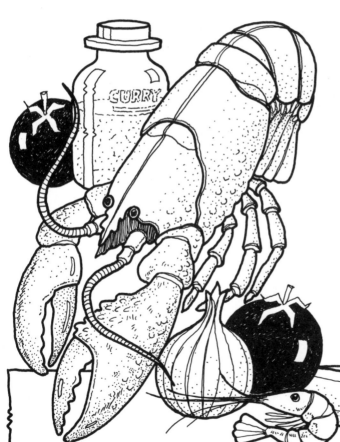

BANANA BREAD

 Cameroon

INGREDIENTS	Imperial	Metric	American
Mashed ripe bananas	6	6	6
Plain flour	1 lb	450 g	4 cups
Baking powder	2 tsp	2 tsp	2 tsp
Bicarbonate of soda	2 tsp	2 tsp	2 tsp
Salt	½ tsp	½ tsp	½ tsp
Eggs	2	2	2
Butter	4 oz	100 g	½ cup
Sugar	4 oz	100 g	½ cup

Grease a bread tin and set the oven at 350 °F/180 ° C/Gas Mark 4. Sift together the flour, salt, baking powder and bicarbonate of soda. Cream the butter and sugar together in a mixing bowl and beat in the eggs one at a time. Blend in the bananas and stir in the flour mixture. Pour into the bread tin and bake for one hour or until cooked, using a toothpick to test if it is cooked. Take bread out of the oven and leave to stand for 10 minutes before turning onto a rack to cool. Serve slices of banana bread with chilled butter.

PLANTAIN WINE

 Cameroon

INGREDIENTS	Imperial	Metric	American
Ripe plantains	6	6	6
Sugar	4 lb	1.8 kg	16 cups
Water	8 pints	4.5 litres	10 pints
Yeast	1 tbsp	1 tbsp	1 tbsp
Sliced bread	1	1	1

Peel and slice plantains, put into a large saucepan and cover with water. Bring to the boil and continue cooking for 10 minutes. Strain the liquid and add the sugar. Allow to cool and pour into a jar. Toast the bread and spread both sides of it with the fresh yeast. Cut it into strips and put into the liquid. Leave the jar uncorked but covered with a clean muslin for 4 to 5 days. Then cork the jar tightly and store for 21 days. Strain and again cork up in the jar for one month. Strain once more and then bottle the wine. Serve when required or leave to mature further.

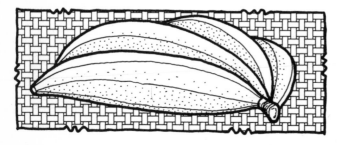

DORO WOT

 Ethiopia

INGREDIENTS	Imperial	Metric	American
Chicken drumsticks, roasted or fried	6	6	6
Onions, sliced	2	2	2
Tomato purée	2 tbsp	2 tbsp	2 tbsp
Berbere (red pepper or chilli)	2 tsp	2 tsp	2 tsp
Black pepper	1 tsp	1 tsp	1 tsp
Butter	1 oz	25 g	⅛ cup
Hard-boiled eggs, shelled	6	6	6
Cubes chicken stock	2	2	2
Salt to taste			

Heat the oil in a saucepan and fry the onion until it is transparent. Stir in the tomato purée, pepper, salt, black pepper and a pint of water and crush in the chicken stock cubes. Simmer for 30 minutes. Add the drumsticks and the eggs and continue to simmer for 10 minutes more. Serve hot with rice. This is a dish fit for an emperor. Find a large bowl and fill it with doro wot making it the centre piece of an attractive buffet.

BEG WOT

Ethiopia

INGREDIENTS	Imperial	Metric	American
Mutton	2 lb	1 kg	2 lb
Butter	4 oz	100 g	½ cup
Paprika or chilli powder	1 tsp	1 tsp	1 tsp
Medium onion	1	1	1
Mixed spice	1 tsp	1 tsp	1 tsp
Tomato purée	1 tbsp	1 tbsp	1 tbsp
For the Side Dish			
Medium cabbage	1	1	1
Salt to taste			

Dice the mutton, wash and boil with salt, a dash of thyme and two slices of onion, until cooked. Melt the butter in another saucepan and lightly fry the meat. Take out the meat and put in a dish. Lightly fry the onion in the same hot oil, add the rest of the ingredients. Add the mutton stock and extra water if necessary. Allow to simmer for 30 minutes. Add the fried mutton and simmer another 10 minutes.

The Side Dish

Wash and shred the cabbage. Boil in boiling salted water but keep cabbage crisp. Alternatively, steam the cabbage. Serve *beg wot* warm with *njera* (bread, page 37) and cabbage.

ABISH

Ethiopia

INGREDIENTS	Imperial	Metric	American
Minced meat	1 lb	450 g	1 lb
Eggs	2	2	2
Medium onions	2	2	2
Medium ripe tomatoes	2	2	2
Butter	4 oz	100 g	½ cup
Berbere (chilli powder)	1 tsp	1 tsp	1 tsp

Finely chop the onions and fry in the butter until tender. Add the sliced tomatoes, *berbere* and salt and stir in the minced meat. Cook for 15 minutes stirring continually. Whisk or beat the eggs and stir into the meat sauce. Reduce the heat and simmer for 5 minutes. Serve with fresh bread.

SHIRO WOT

Ethiopia

INGREDIENTS	Imperial	Metric	American
Raw dry groundnuts	8 oz	225 g	2 cups
Butter	2 oz	50 g	¼ cup
Tomato purée	1 tbsp	1 tbsp	1 tbsp
Small onion	1	1	1
Mixed spices to taste	½ tsp	½ tsp	½ tsp
Salt and pepper to taste			

Shell groundnuts, clean and grind into flour. Put the other ingredients into a saucepan with a pint of water and bring to the boil. Simmer for 30 minutes. Serve with fluffy white rice or *njera*. This is not dissimilar from the regular groundnut stew. So add boiled young chicken or fresh fish to Shiro Wot, with a cube of chicken stock to make it tastier.

KITFO

Ethiopia

INGREDIENTS	Imperial	Metric	American
Prime beef (or liver)	1 lb	450 g	1 lb
Butter	4 oz	100 g	½ cup
Hot chilli sauce	2 tsp	2 tsp	2 tsp
Mixed spices	1 tsp	1 tsp	1 tsp
Medium onion	1	1	1
Vinegar	2 tbsp	2 tbsp	2 tbsp
Salt to taste			

Finely mince the beef or liver and slice the onion thinly. Mix all the ingredients in a bowl. Serve mixture tastily on plates, garnished with fresh salad with lacings of tomato ketchup. Note that there has been no cooking; the beef or liver is served raw. If you are unable to eat raw meat or liver, lightly fry in a little butter or grill or broil lightly before serving.

Pepper Chicken—page 29
with Yam Balls—page 81

AKOTONSHI

Ghana

INGREDIENTS	Imperial	Metric	American
Land crabs	12	12	12
Small green sweet pepper, sliced	1	1	1
Small red sweet pepper, sliced	1	1	1
Large onion, finely chopped	1	1	1
Medium tomatoes, finely chopped	4	4	4
Tomato purée	1 tbsp	1 tbsp	1 tbsp
Ground ginger	1 tbsp	1 tbsp	1 tbsp
Cayenne pepper	1 tsp	1 tsp	1 tsp
Mixed herbs	1 tsp	1 tsp	1 tsp
Crushed fresh ginger	1 tsp	1 tsp	1 tsp
Fresh shrimps	8 oz	225 g	1 cup
Cooking oil	4 tbsp	4 tbsp	4 tbsp
Lime or lemon, fresh	1	1	1
Breadcrumbs	6 tbsp	6 tbsp	6 tbsp

Wash crabs thoroughly and rub with lime juice. Combine crabs, one pint of water, salt and the crushed ginger in a saucepan and boil for 30 minutes. Remove the shells, scrub and keep them. Extract as much flesh as possible from the crabs.

Heat the oil and lightly fry the shrimps and at five-minute intervals add the onion, ginger, peppers, tomatoes and the herbs. Cook for 20 minutes and then stir in the crab meat and cook for a further 15 minutes.

Fill the crab shells with the mixture and sprinkle with a generous covering of breadcrumbs. Arrange *akotonshi* on a baking tray and put under a hot grill or broiler to brown the tops. Serve hot with fried *yam* or boiled *cassava*.

NJERA

Ethiopia

INGREDIENTS	Imperial	Metric	American
Tef *flour (Ethiopian grain)*	1 lb	450 g	4 cups
Warm milky water	½ pint	250 ml	1¼ cups
Dry yeast	1 oz	25 g	1 oz
Sugar	1 tbsp	1 tbsp	1 tbsp

Stir first the sugar and then the yeast into the milky water. Allow to stand for about 20 minutes or until the yeast water becomes frothy. Put the *tef* flour into a mixing bowl. Mix in the frothy yeast water. Knead well to a stiff dough. Cover up and allow to rise for 30 minutes. Set oven for 400 °F/200 °C/Gas Mark 6. Grease a baking tray or tins, mould the dough into desired small shapes, place in trays or tins and cover with a clean muslin or polythene sheet for about 40 minutes to allow dough to rise.

Bake for 30—40 minutes. Allow to cool on a wire rack and store to serve with sauces (*wot*) or butter.

Kidney with Rice Balls—page 32

GALI FOTO

Ghana

INGREDIENTS	Imperial	Metric	American
Gali	1 lb	450 g	1 lb
Large ripe tomatoes, chopped	2	2	2
Large onion, chopped	1	1	1
Tomato purée	1 tbsp	1 tbsp	1 tbsp
Green or red sweet pepper, chopped	1	1	1
Eggs	4	4	4
Chilli powder or cayenne pepper	1 tsp	1 tsp	1 tsp
Ground ginger	½ tsp	½ tsp	½ tsp
Fresh lobsters or shrimps, shelled	½ lb	225 g	½ lb
Corned beef or salmon, tin	½	½	½
Cooking oil	6 tbsp	6 tbsp	6 tbsp

Sprinkle the *gali* with salted water and leave to absorb the water, but do not saturate. Heat oil in a saucepan and fry the onion until light brown, add the tomatoes, peppers, salt and ginger. Whisk (beat) the eggs lightly and gradually stir into the sauce. Crush the corned beef or salmon and mix it in. Gradually stir in the soaked *gali*. Reduce heat and allow *gali* to warm through for five minutes. Heat a little oil in a frying pan, add a pinch of ground ginger and fry the lobsters or shrimps in it until cooked.

Serve *gali foto* hot, garnished with the lobsters.

Gali, pronounced *gari* in some parts of West Africa, is a coarse flour made from cassava, an edible tuberous root which is one of Africa's staple foods. Although *gali foto* is a speciality of Ghana and Togo, it is now a favourite dish in other parts of West Africa, wherever the Ghanaians and Togolese have settled.

GINGER FRIED FISH

Ghana

INGREDIENTS	Imperial	Metric	American
Rock fish or mullet	4 lb	1.8 kg	4 lb
Ground ginger	1 tbsp	1 tbsp	1 tbsp
Onion, ground or liquidized	1	1	1
Ground red pepper	1 tsp	1 tsp	1 tsp
Salt to taste			
Cooking oil to fry			

Clean fish and divide into cutlets. Put fish in a bowl and mix with the ginger, onion, tomato and salt. Allow to stand for about 15 minutes. Heat oil in a frying pan and fry fish, ensuring that all sides of the cutlets are cooked. Arrange decoratively on a platter and garnish with parsley and tomatoes.

Serve with freshly boiled yam, rice or on a bed of fresh salad.

GHANAIAN FOWL

Ghana

INGREDIENTS	Imperial	Metric	American
Duck	1	1	1
Shredded meat or chicken or corned beef	1 lb	450 g	1 lb
Cooked yam or cassava	1 lb	450 g	1 lb
Tomatoes, chopped	½ lb	225 g	½ lb
Medium onion, chopped	1	1	1
Groundnut oil	2 tbsp	2 tbsp	2 tbsp
Salt and pepper to taste			

Heat the oil and fry the shredded meat, onion and tomatoes. Mash the *yam* and stir it in. Leave on one side having turned off the heat.

Bone the duck, clean and salt it inside out. Stuff the bird with the mixture, then, with a needle and thread, sew the duck into shape. Place in a large saucepan, cover and steam for about 1½ hours over low heat. When done rub the bird with butter and roast in an oven for 30 minutes until golden brown. Serve slices of roast duck with *jollof* rice (page 62).

GROUNDNUT STEW

Ghana

INGREDIENTS	Imperial	Metric	American
Roasted groundnuts, puréed	4 oz	100 g	½ cup
Groundnut oil	1 tbsp	1 tbsp	1 tbsp
Tomato purée	1 tbsp	1 tbsp	1 tbsp
Cayenne or chilli powder	1 tsp	1 tsp	1 tsp
Small onion, ground or liquidized	1	1	1
Chicken, mutton or pork	2 lb	1 kg	2 lb
Mixed spice	½ tsp	½ tsp	½ tsp
Salt to taste			

Chop or dice meat and boil with salt, mixed herbs and two slices of onion for 30 minutes. Add two cups of water and the rest of the ingredients (except groundnuts) and continue to cook for 20 minutes. Stir in the peanut purée and simmer for 10 minutes. Serve hot with fluffy white rice.

Groundnuts, popularly called peanuts in Europe and America, grow profusely in the savannah regions of Africa. These highly versatile nuts grow below the ground, hence we call them ground nuts. They provide us with cooking oil and you can eat them cooked, roasted, or raw. You can make them into cookies or grind the roasted peanuts for use as butter.

TATALI

Ghana

INGREDIENTS	Imperial	Metric	American
Maize flour (cornmeal)	1 lb	450 g	3 cups
Over-ripe plantains	2 lb	1 kg	2 lb
Medium onion	1	1	1
Ground ginger	1 tsp	1 tsp	1 tsp
Hot fresh peppers, ground	1 tsp	1 tsp	1 tsp
Palmnut oil, to fry	8 fl. oz	200 ml	1 cup
Salt to taste			

Pound the over-ripe plantains in a mortar (or cut into small pieces and liquidize). Stir in the maize flour and the other ingredients. Heat the palmnut oil, scoop up a bit of the mixture at a time and put into the hot oil and, depending on the size of the frying pan, fry up to ten scoops at a time. Fry for about 5 minutes; flick each *tatali* onto the other side to fry. Press each one flat with the back of a stirring spoon and continue to fry until crisp and golden.

Serve hot with well cooked beans (red or black-eyed beans), with rich fish pepper sauce (*yoyo*, page 26).

PONKIE

Ghana

INGREDIENTS	Imperial	Metric	American
Ponkie (*pumpkin*), diced	2 lb	1 kg	2 lb
Medium aubergine (egg plant)	1	1	1
Beef, minced	1 lb	450 g	1 lb
Green pepper, chopped	1	1	1
Medium onion, chopped	1	1	1
Large ripe tomatoes, chopped	2	2	2
Cayenne or chilli powder	½ tsp	½ tsp	½ tsp
Coriander powder	½ tsp	½ tsp	½ tsp
Cooking oil	2 tbsp	2 tbsp	2 tbsp
Salt to taste			

Dice the aubergine and soak in salted water. Heat the oil in a saucepan and lightly fry the onion. Add the minced meat, salt and coriander and cook for 10 minutes. Stir in the onion, peppers, tomatoes and pumpkin. Drain the aubergine and stir it in. Reduce heat and simmer for 20 minutes. Serve hot with boiled *yam*, *cassava* or rice.

Aubergines are known as 'Garden eggs' in Africa.

NKRAKRA

Ghana

INGREDIENTS	Imperial	Metric	American
Yam, *peeled and diced*	1 lb	450 g	1 lb
Fresh or smoked fish	1 lb	450 g	1 lb
Tomato purée	1 tbsp	1 tbsp	1 tbsp
Small onion, thinly sliced	1	1	1
Cooking oil	1 tbsp	1 tbsp	1 tbsp
Fresh chilli pepper, ground	½ tbsp	½ tbsp	½ tbsp

Simmer the chilli pepper, tomatoes, onion, salt and oil in 1 pint/500 ml/2½ cups of water for 45 minutes or until the smell of raw pepper is no longer there. Sieve the soup into another saucepan, put in the *yam* and cook until *yam* is soft but not mashed. Add the fish and simmer for 20 minutes. Serve hot.

If fresh fish is used, clean and sprinkle with salt and a dash of lime juice and put aside until needed.

This is the famous African 'pepper soup' called by different names in other parts of Africa. It is ideal for a sick person with no appetite for solid food.

KENKEY

Ghana

INGREDIENTS	Imperial	Metric	American
Maize flour (cornmeal)	2 lb	1 kg	6 cups
Pepper Fish			
Fresh fish	2 lb	1 kg	2 lb
Fresh pepper, ground	2 tsp	2 tsp	2 tsp
Tomato purée	1 tbsp	1 tbsp	1 tbsp
Onion, ground	2 tsp	2 tsp	2 tsp
Oil	1 tbsp	1 tbsp	1 tbsp
Salt to taste			

Prepare *kanke* a week or two before you need it or buy ready-made corn dough. Mix the cornmeal (maize flour) with sufficient water to make a fairly stiff dough. Tie up dough in a muslin and suspend in a pan, cover and allow to ferment for a week or two. Knead well and mould into small portions inside corn sheaves or in aluminium foil. Steam in a cooking pot for about an hour or until well cooked. Serve hot with pepper fish.

Pepper Fish Method:

In a saucepan, heat the oil and fry the fresh fish until cooked and crisp. Mix the peppers, onion and tomato purée with salt, garnish the fish with it.

ABOLOO

Ghana

INGREDIENTS	Imperial	Metric	American
Maize flour (cornmeal)	1 lb	450 g	3 cups
Milk or milk and water	1 pint	500 ml	2½ cups
Sugar	4 oz	100 g	½ cup

Mix the cornmeal flour with part of the milk and water and the sugar into a fairly thick paste. In a deep saucepan, heat the rest of the milk and half pint of water and bring to the boil.

Stir in the flour paste into the boiling water to slightly stiff paste. Cook for about 10 minutes, wrap small portions in banana leaves and allow to cool and set. Alternatively, use jelly moulds. Serve cold on its own or crushed into milk with sugar.

DIOMBRE

Ivory Coast

INGREDIENTS	Imperial	Metric	American
Dry okra, well crushed in mortar	4 oz	100 g	¼ lb
Prime beef or mutton	1 lb	450 g	1 lb
Tomato purée	1 tbsp	1 tbsp	1 tbsp
Medium-sized ripe fresh tomatoes	3	3	3
Medium onion	1	1	1
Chilli powder	1 tsp	1 tsp	1 tsp
Butter	2 oz	50 g	¼ cup
Pinch of thyme			
Salt to taste			
Oil	3 tbsp	3 tbsp	3 tbsp

Cut the meat into small pieces and rinse it; boil with salt and thyme until tender. In a saucepan heat the oil and lightly fry the meat. Chop the onion and fresh tomatoes and add to the meat, let it cook for 5 minutes. Stir in the rest of the ingredients with a cup of water. Cover the pot and simmer until the meat is well cooked, and the chilli cooked. Stir in the dry crushed okra and continue to simmer for a further 5—10 minutes. Serve with *foufou* (*fufu*, page 13) or cassava or rice.

FUTU

Ivory Coast

INGREDIENTS	Imperial	Metric	American
Meat	2 lb	1 kg	2 lb
Dry fish	1 lb	450 g	1 lb
Fresh crisp okra, finely chopped	8 oz	225 g	½ lb
Fresh ground chilli powder	½ tsp	½ tsp	½ tsp
Medium onion, ground	1	1	1
Chicken stock, made from chicken cube	1 pint	500 ml	2½ cups
Tomato purée	1 tbsp	1 tbsp	1 tbsp
Garden eggs, egg plant, diced	2	2	2
or Aubergine, diced	1	1	1
Roasted groundnuts, puréed	4 oz	100 g	½ cup
Palmnut oil	4 fl. oz	100 ml	½ cup
Salt to taste			

Boil the meat with salt and a slice of onion for 20 minutes. Add the chilli powder, tomato purée, onion, palmnut oil, chicken stock and cook for 20 minutes. Stir in the groundnut purée and garden eggs or aubergine and simmer for 10 minutes. Add the fish and the okra and continue to simmer a further 10 minutes. Serve hot with *foufou* (*fufu*, page 13).

KUKU

Kenya

INGREDIENTS	Imperial	Metric	American
Chicken	1	1	1
Curry powder	1 tbsp	1 tbsp	1 tbsp
Large onion, sliced	1	1	1
Mixed spice	1 tsp	1 tsp	1 tsp
Cornflour (cornstarch)	1 tbsp	1 tbsp	1 tbsp
Cooking oil	8 fl. oz	200 ml	1 cup
Salt to taste			

Clean chicken and cut into portions. Wash well and season with the spice, salt and onion. Cover and leave to stand for about two hours. Heat the oil and fry chicken portions, keeping the heat low to allow chicken to brown well. Remove chicken and put in a saucepan with two cups of water. Simmer until chicken is cooked. Stir the curry powder and cornflour into the leftover oil in the frying pan adding a little of the chicken stock to make a smooth gravy. Pour this over the chicken, cover and simmer for 10 minutes. Serve hot with *irio* (page 16) or rice.

ATIEKE

Ivory Coast

INGREDIENTS	Imperial	Metric	American
Cassava grains (white garri, bought ready-made)	1 lb	450 g	4 cups
Vegetable Sauce			
Beef or mutton, diced	2 lb	1 kg	2 lb
Ripe tomatoes	4	4	4
Medium carrots	4	4	4
Onion	1	1	1
Tomato purée	5 oz	125 g	⅝ cup
Medium turnips	2	2	2
Aubergine (eggplant)	1	1	1
Cauliflower	½	½	½
Cabbage	½	½	½
Small swede (rutabaga)	1	1	1
Green beans	1 lb	1 lb	1 lb
Parsley sprigs	2	2	2
Garlic clove, crushed	1	1	1
Cayenne pepper	1 tsp	1 tsp	1 tsp
Cooking oil	8 fl. oz	200 ml	1 cup

Bring the meat to the boil with half the onion, salt and garlic. Simmer it while you heat the oil in a large heavy pan. Fry the rest of the onion, tomatoes, tomato purée and seasoning. Cook for 15 minutes, stirring occasionally. Wash clean and chop the rest of the vegetables and stir them in with the rest of the ingredients and the meat. Cover and cook gently for 45 minutes to an hour, until the sauce is thick and the meat tender.

Mix the cassava grains with a little cold water into soft granules. Stir in a dash of salt and serve with the vegetable sauce. The dish is a cassava variation of the Senegal couscous.

Note that garri has not been steamed at all, unlike couscous. An alternative to the couscous sauce is pepper sauce with lots of sliced onion and sliced fresh tomatoes. Add 2 ozs/50 g/¼ cup of crushed corned beef to the pepper sauce.

MEAT GRAVY

Kenya

INGREDIENTS	Imperial	Metric	American
Beef or mutton, diced	2 lbs	1 kg	2 lbs
Kimbo (butter)	1 tbsp	1 tbsp	1 tbsp
Large onion, sliced	1	1	1
Large ripe tomato, sliced	1	1	1
Tomato purée	1 tbsp	1 tbsp	1 tbsp
White pepper	1 tsp	1 tsp	1 tsp
Pinch of mixed herbs			
Salt to taste			

Boil meat with salt, two slices of onion, and mixed herbs. Melt the *kimbo* in a saucepan and lightly fry the onion, add the meat and stock and the rest of the ingredients. Cover and simmer for 20 minutes. Serve with *irio* (page 16).

BANANA CAKE

Liberia

INGREDIENTS	Imperial	Metric	American
Mashed bananas	6	6	6
Eggs	3	3	3
Sugar	6 oz	150 g	¾ cup
Butter	4 oz	100 g	½ cup
Buttermilk	8 fl. oz	200 ml	1 cup
Salt	1 tsp	1 tsp	1 tsp
Plain flour	1 lb	450 g	4 cups
Baking powder	2 tsp	2 tsp	2 tsp
Bicarbonate of soda	2 tsp	2 tsp	2 tsp
Salt	1 tsp	1 tsp	1 tsp
Mixed dried fruit (currants, raisins, sultanas)	2 oz	50 g	½ cup

Set oven at 350 °F/180 °C/Gas Mark 4. Sift flour, baking powder, salt and soda together and add the sugar. Mix in the butter, half the buttermilk and the mashed bananas. Mix in the rest of the buttermilk and the dried fruit. Grease and lightly flour a 10 in./ 25 cm cake tin. Turn the cake mixture into the tin and bake in the centre of the oven for 45 minutes or until cooked, using a toothpick to test. Turn onto a rack to cool.

LE COUSCOUS D'ARABIE

Morocco

INGREDIENTS	Imperial	Metric	American
Couscous	1 lb	450 g	1 lb
Roasting chicken portions	6	6	6
Chicken giblets, minced	4 oz	100 g	¼ lb
Mutton, minced	2 oz	50 g	2 oz
Chick peas, soaked overnight	4 oz	100 g	½ cup
Carrots	2	2	2
Small turnips, diced	2	2	2
Onion	1	1	1
Celery sticks	2	2	2
Leeks	2	2	2
Small cauliflower	1	1	1
Small cabbage	1	1	1
Swede (rutabaga)	½	½	½
Tomato purée	4 tbsp	4 tbsp	4 tbsp
Eggs	2	2	2
Mixed spice	1 tsp	1 tsp	1 tsp
Cooking oil	6 tbsp	6 tbsp	6 tbsp
Salted butter	2 oz	50 g	¼ cup
Sweet red pepper, chopped	1	1	1
Potatoes	4	4	4

For best results, use a *couscoussier* to prepare this meal (or its equivalent which is a three-piece steamer consisting of a saucepan with a steamer and lid). In the pot, heat the cooking oil and brown the chicken. Mix the minced mutton and giblets with the eggs and spices, mould into small meatballs and place them in the chicken pot. Fry until brown.

Add the onion, pepper and tomato purée and stir gently. Add the salt, two glasses of water and the washed chick peas. Cover pot and simmer for about 20 minutes. Wash and dice the vegetables and stir into the sauce. Dampen the *couscous* with a little cold water, mix gently and pour into the steamer. Place the steamer over the saucepan and cover with the lid. Leave both the sauce and the *couscous* to cook for about 40 minutes. Remove the steamer and turn *couscous* into a large mixing bowl. Sprinkle with a little cold water and, with a wooden spoon, break any lumps in *couscous* to get a grain-like looseness. Turn back into the steamer and return to the pot. Cover and steam some 20 minutes more. Turn the *couscous* into a large serving dish, gently stir in the salted butter with a pinch of cinnamon and a sprinkling of warm water to moisten it. With a spatula, tease the couscous into a mound pour the vegetable sauce over it and garnish with the chicken and meatballs. Serve warm.

MOROCCAN ORANGES

Morocco

INGREDIENTS	Imperial	Metric	American
Oranges, peeled	6	6	6
Icing (confectioner) sugar	3 tbsp	3 tbsp	3 tbsp
Powdered cinnamon	½ tsp	½ tsp	½ tsp
Orange flower water	2 tsp	2 tsp	2 tsp

Remove the white pith from the oranges and slice them. Put the slices in a shallow dish and sprinkle with the orange flower water, the icing sugar and the cinnamon. Leave to stand for 1½ hours, turning the slices over from time to time. Serve chilled.

ASARO

Nigeria

INGREDIENTS	Imperial	Metric	American
Dry smoked fish	½ lb	225 g	½ lb
Yam, peeled and diced	4 lb	1.8 kg	4 lb
Tomato purée, 5 oz/125 g can	1	1	1
Fresh ripe tomatoes	4	4	4
Small onions	2	2	2
Chilli powder	1 tsp	1 tsp	1 tsp
Groundnut oil or palmnut oil	6 tbsp	6 tbsp	6 tbsp
Ground crayfish	1 tbsp	1 tbsp	1 tbsp
Cube chicken stock	1	1	1
Salt to taste			

Wash *yam* and boil in a saucepan with one onion, sliced, salt, one tablespoon oil and 1⅗ pints/ 600 ml/3 cups of water. Grind or liquidize the fresh tomatoes and one onion, add to the *yam*, stir in the chilli powder, tomato purée, chicken stock, crayfish and cooking oil. Cover pot and reduce the heat. Simmer gently until *yam* is cooked and soft. Mash half the *yam* with a wooden spoon and stir gently to distribute the lumps evenly. Stir in the washed boned dry fish, and allow to simmer 10 minutes more. Serve warm.

WAINA

Nigeria

INGREDIENTS	Imperial	Metric	American
Per person			
Eggs	*2*	*2*	*2*
Cooking oil to deep fry	*8 fl. oz*	*200 ml*	*1 cup*
Salt and pepper to taste			

Whisk (beat or whip) eggs thoroughly, adding a tablespoon of water to two eggs, and a pinch of salt. Heat oil in a deep frying pan. When oil is hot, pour a ladleful of egg at a time into the hot oil and fry until golden and crisp. It should look like a crisp sponge. Take out of the oil, drain and spread on a flat dish. Continue to fry the egg in the same manner until it is used up. Serve *waina* hot with fresh baked bread.

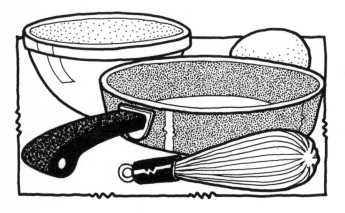

WAKE-EWA

Nigeria

INGREDIENTS	Imperial	Metric	American
Black-eyed beans	*1 lb*	*450 g*	*1 lb*
Sugar	*1 tbsp*	*1 tbsp*	*1 tbsp*
Salt to taste			
Pepper Sauce			
Tomatoes	*3*	*3*	*3*
Onion	*1*	*1*	*1*
Groundnut oil	*6 tbsp*	*6 tbsp*	*6 tbsp*
Chilli powder	*1 tsp*	*1 tsp*	*1 tsp*
Dash of thyme and coriander powder			
Salt to taste			

Liquidize the tomatoes with half the onion and slice the rest. Heat the oil and fry the onion slices. Combine the spices with the tomato mixture and stir into the hot oil. Cook for 25 minutes, stirring constantly.

Pour beans into a colander and wash thoroughly. Turn beans into a deep saucepan with 1½ pints/750 ml/3¾ cups of water and boil over a low fire for 30 minutes. Pour through a colander, rinse again and turn back into the washed pot with ¾ pint/375 ml/1⅞ cups of water, the sugar and salt. Cover pot and simmer steadily until beans are cooked and quite soft. Serve hot with pepper sauce and/or *garri* (grain-like *cassava* flour).

MOIN-MOIN

Nigeria

INGREDIENTS	Imperial	Metric	American
Black-eyed beans, skinned	1 lb	450 g	1 lb
Large onion	1	1	1
Chilli powder	2 tsp	2 tsp	2 tsp
Tomato purée	2 tbsp	2 tbsp	2 tbsp
Fresh tomatoes	2	2	2
Ground crayfish	2 tbsp	2 tbsp	2 tbsp
Palmnut or cooking oil	8 fl. oz	200 ml	1 cup
Salt to taste			
A bundle of banana leaves, foil or bread tins to steam			

To skin beans: soak for 30 minutes and then drain off the water. Using both hands with a squeezing, washing action, peel the skins off the beans. Cover with water and the skins will float and can be collected in a sieve or strainer as the water is drained off into a second bowl. Repeat the sequence to skin the remaining beans.

Soak skinned beans until very soft, grind or liquidize and pour into a mixing bowl. Chop the onion and fresh tomatoes and stir into the bean purée. Add the salt, crayfish, chilli powder and tomato purée. Pour 4 fl. oz/100 ml/½ cup of hot water into the oil, and then pour both into the beans. Mix well. Shape two leaves at a time into an envelope, put into it two tablespoons of the bean mixture and arrange on a steamer. Put the steamer over a pot of boiling water, cover with a lid and steam steadily for one hour.

UKPO

Nigeria

INGREDIENTS	Imperial	Metric	American
Green plantain flour	1 lb	450 g	1 lb
Over-ripe plantain	4 lb	2 kg	4 lb
Fresh ripe peppers, ground	2 oz	50 g	½ cup
Small onion, ground	1	1	1
Palmnut oil	4 fl. oz	100 g	½ cup
Salt to taste			

Pound the over-ripe plantain in a mortar and put in a mixing bowl. Stir in the green plantain flour, and the rest of the ingredients. Mix well, put small portions in leaf wrappings (or in foil) and arrange on a steamer in a cooking pot half filled with water.

Steam for about an hour or until cooked. Test by sticking a toothpick into one; if the pick comes out clean, the *ukpo* is cooked. Serve on its own, warm.

RICH MOIN-MOIN

Nigeria

INGREDIENTS	Imperial	Metric	American
Quantity of basic moin-moin (page 49)			
Chicken stock cube	*1*	*1*	*1*
Combination of fresh shelled prawns, chicken meat, bits of salmon, sliced sausages, sliced boiled eggs, onion, diced corned beef	*1 lb*	*450 g*	*1 lb*

Thoroughly grease a large bread tin. Prepare *moin-moin* as shown on page 49, incorporating the chicken stock cube into the basic mixture. Do not steam the *moin-moin*, but pour a cup of the mix into the bottom of the bread tin. Cover with any of the fillings and continue making alternate layers of bean purée and filling until the tin is three quarters full, finishing with a layer of bean purée. Cover tin with foil, put on the top shelf of the oven and bake for 1½ hours at 350 °F/180 °C/Gas Mark 4. If you have a cooking pot large enough to take bread tins you might find it economical to steam the *moin-moin* by putting the tin in a steaming bag and boiling it in the pot with 1½ pints/750 ml/3¾ cups of water. Add more water if necessary. A knife pushed into the *moin-moin* should come out clean when it is cooked.

Rich *moin-moin* is a very popular party dish throughout West Africa.

DANWAKE

Nigeria

INGREDIENTS	Imperial	Metric	American
Dry bean flour	*½ lb*	*225 g*	*½ lb*
Kuka powder (baobab leaves)	*1 tbsp*	*1 tbsp*	*1 tbsp*
Small piece potash or rock salt	*1*	*1*	*1*
Warm water	*8 fl. oz*	*200 ml*	*1 cup*

Dissolve potash in warm water. Mix bean flour and *kuka* powder in a mixing bowl. Make a well in the centre of flour and pour in the potash water to make a slightly stiff dough. Cover and leave on one side for 20 minutes. Boil 2 pints/1 litre/5 cups of water in a deep saucepan, mould mixture a little at a time and drop dumplings of it into the boiling water. Continue making the dumplings until the mixture has been used up. Partly cover pot and cook for about 40 minutes. Extract *danwake* from boiling water with a strainer. Serve hot sprinkled with salt and red pepper powder.

LANSUR SALAD

 Nigeria

INGREDIENTS	Imperial	Metric	American
Lansur, (parsley-like vegetable which tastes like cress)	1 lb	450 g	1 lb
Kuli-kuli, pounded	1 lb	450 g	1 lb
Red sweet pepper	1	1	1
Green sweet pepper	1	1	1
Small onion	1	1	1
Chilli powder	½ tsp	½ tsp	½ tsp
Mixed spice	1 tsp	1 tsp	1 tsp
Salt to taste			
Kuli-kuli			
Roasted groundnuts	2 lb	1 kg	2 lb
Warm water	4 fl. oz	100 ml	½ cup
Groundnut oil to fry			

Grind the cleaned groundnuts; knead the resulting paste thoroughly to extract all the oil, working in the warm water by degrees to help the process. When as much oil as possible has been squeezed out, shape the paste into small flat cakes and deep fry in the extracted oil. If there is not enough add more groundnut oil.

Wash, drain and finely chop the *lansur* and put it in a mixing bowl. Thinly slice the onion and peppers, discarding the seeds. Add all the ingredients to the *lansur* and mix well. Serve immediately.

IKOKORE

 Nigeria

INGREDIENTS	Imperial	Metric	American
Water-yam	2 lb	1 kg	2 lb
Tomato purée	2 tbsp	2 tbsp	2 tbsp
Medium onion, ground	1	1	1
Ground fresh peppers or chilli powder	2 tsp	2 tsp	2 tsp
Ogiri or locustbean	½ tsp	½ tsp	½ tsp
or meat/chicken stock cube	1	1	1
Palmnut oil	4 fl. oz	100 ml	½ cup
Smoked dry fish	1 lb	450 g	1 lb
Salt to taste			

Peel *yam*, wash and grate. Leave grated *yam* in a bowl. In a deep cooking pot, combine all the other ingredients except the fish and simmer with ½ pint/ 250 ml/1¼ cups of water for one hour.

Wash the fish well and break into a dish, taking out as many of the bones as possible. Add the fish to the soup. Then using your hand, whisk (mix) the grated *yam*, add a dash of salt. If *yam* is too watery, stir in a little wheat flour. Now take a small scoop at a time with the hand and drop it into the soup making dumplings in this way until the grated *yam* is used up. Reduce the heat, cover the pot and simmer gently for about 30—40 minutes or until *yam* is cooked. Serve warm.

BIRABISKO DA TAUSHE

Nigeria

INGREDIENTS	Imperial	Metric	American
Polished jero (millet), coarsely crushed	1 lb	450 g	1 lb
Taushe			
Brisket of beef	2 lb	1 kg	2 lb
Large onion	1	1	1
Yakua greens	1 lb	450 g	1 lb
Pumpkin	1½ lb	675 g	1½ lb
Raw groundnuts, puréed	8 oz	225 g	½ lb
Tomatoes	2 lb	1 kg	2 lb
Chilli powder	1 tsp	1 tsp	1 tsp
Daddawa (locust bean)	2 oz	50 g	2 oz
Cooking oil	4 tbsp	4 tbsp	4 tbsp
Salt to taste			
Butter	1 lb	450 g	1 lb

Put butter in a small earthenware pot with a pinch of salt and a slice of onion. Simmer over a very low fire until the oil is clear and onion slices are golden brown. Take off heat and allow to cool on one side.

Meanwhile prepare *taushe* soup. Chop brisket and combine meat, tomatoes, salt, pepper, onion and other seasoning and cooking oil in a heavy pan with 16 fl. oz/400 ml/2 cups of water. Cook for 30 minutes. Add the pumpkin and cook for a further 20 minutes. Add the groundnuts and chopped greens, reduce the heat and cook for 20 minutes more.

In a deep pot, boil 2 pints of water, stir in the crushed millet grains quickly. Cover pot and allow to simmer over a very low fire until water has been absorbed and millet is cooked and soft.

Serve hot with *taushe* soup (page 19) dressed with spoonfuls of butter.

CASSAVA NA CALABAR

Nigeria

INGREDIENTS	Imperial	Metric	American
Fresh cassava	2 lb	1 kg	2 lb
Salted smoked herrings	2 lb	1 kg	2 lb

Peel the *cassava*, cut into pieces, wash well, put in a saucepan and cover with water. Cover pot and cook on medium fire until half-cooked. Reduce the water, and arrange cutlets of salted herrings on top of the *cassava*. Cover pot and simmer until *cassava* is well cooked and soft. It will have absorbed some of the salt from the herrings. Serve hot with butter.

MASAH

 Nigeria

INGREDIENTS	Imperial	Metric	American
Ground corn meal flour **or** a mixture of ground rice and flour sifted	1 lb	450 g	3 cups
with 4 tsp baking powder	1 lb	450 g	3 cups
Oil to fry	8 fl. oz	200 ml	1 cup
Sugar	1 tbsp	1 tbsp	1 tbsp
Dry yeast	2 tsp	2 tsp	2 tsp
Warm milky water	6 fl. oz	150 ml	¾ cup

Dissolve the sugar in the warm milky water in a mixing bowl. Mix the yeast into the water and cover bowl. Allow to stand until mixture becomes frothy. Mix in the corn meal flour and leave for about 30 minutes to rise. Mix well into a soft slightly dropping consistency. Using a very small frying pan, heat a tablespoon of oil, just enough to cover the base of pan. Fry a spoonful of the mixture at a time. Halfway through cooking, turn *masah* to fry the other side. Fry on low heat to allow *masah* to cook without burning. Continue the process until the mixture is used up. Serve *masah* hot with wild honey or vegetable (*taushe*) soup (page 19).

AGBONO SOUP

 Nigeria

INGREDIENTS	Imperial	Metric	American
Goat meat	1 lb	450 g	1 lb
Dry smoked fish	1 lb	450 g	1 lb
Agbono *nuts, puréed*	4 oz	100 g	¼ lb
Ground fresh peppers	1 tsp	1 tsp	1 tsp
or Chilli powder	1 tsp	1 tsp	1 tsp
Tomato purée	1 tbsp	1 tbsp	1 tbsp
Medium onion, puréed	1	1	1
Bitterleaf leaves	2	2	2
Fresh okra	2 oz	50 g	2 oz
Palmnut oil	8 fl. oz	200 ml	1 cup
Crayfish, ground	2 tbsp	2 tbsp	2 tbsp
Salt to taste			

In a large pot, boil the meat with salt and onion. Fry the meat in hot palmnut oil until brown and put on one side in a dish. Pour the hot oil into the large pot and combine with it the tomato purée, onion, pepper and salt. Cook for about 20 minutes.

Meanwhile, crush the bitterleaf and wash out most of the bitterness. Add to the soup and continue to cook. Chop the onion finely. Wash and bone the fish. Add the fried meat, fish, and okra to the soup, and cook for 10 minutes. Stir in the *agbono* and reduce the heat. Simmer for 10 minutes. Stir in the crayfish and continue to simmer a further 10 minutes. Serve hot with *ine-oka* (page 14), *fufu* (page 13) or pounded *yam* (page 14).

ACHA

Nigeria

INGREDIENTS	Imperial	Metric	American
Acha (tiny grains, much smaller than mustard	1 lb	450 g	3 cups
Tin tomato purée, 5 oz/125 g	1	1	1
Medium onion, ground	1	1	1
Meat	8 oz	225 g	½ lb
Dry smoked fish	1 lb	450 g	1 lb
Ground pepper or chilli powder	1 tsp	1 tsp	1 tsp
Fresh tomatoes, sliced	8 oz	225 g	½ lb
Groundnut oil	4 fl. oz	100 ml	½ cup
Salt to taste			

Dice the meat, heat oil and fry meat with salt and a slice of onion until brown. Take the meat out of the oil and leave aside in a dish. Add a pint of water and the rest of the ingredients, except the fish and the acha, to the hot oil. Cover pot and simmer for 20 minutes. Wash and bone the fish and leave aside in a dish.

Acha grains usually have a lot of fine particules of sand which should be extracted from the acha by 'pan-washing' or, more appropriately, 'calabash-washing'. You need two small calabashes (bowls made from gourds); put acha in one of the calabashes and cover with water. Firsh wash acha by rubbing between the palms. Drain off water and cover with fresh clean water. Pan-wash acha from one into the other calabash. Throw away the fine sand at the bottom of the first calabash. Repeat action from one calabash to the other until no more sand is left in the acha.

Add the fried meat and the fish to the sauce and simmer for 15 minutes. Stir in the acha into the sauce. Reduce the heat and simmer over very low heat until acha is soft and has absorbed all the moisture. While cooking, add small quantities of water if necessary. Serve warm.

FUNKASO

Nigeria

INGREDIENTS	Imperial	Metric	American
Jero (millet) flour	1 lb	450 g	4 cups
Butter	2 oz	50 g	¼ cup
Oil to deep-fry			
Caster sugar to coat			

In a mixing bowl, melt the butter in 1 pint/500 ml/2½ cups of hot water. Stir in the flour rapidly to make a runny consistency. Allow to stand for up to 4 hours.

Heat the oil in a shallow frying pan. Mix the mixture well, and with a large spoon, scoop up portions into the hot oil and fry until golden and crisp. It should spread like a pancake. Put all the funkaso on a tray and serve coated in caster sugar.

FURA

Nigeria

INGREDIENTS	Imperial	Metric	American
Jero (millet)	2 lb	1 kg	2 lb
Mixed spices: peppercorn, chilli, cloves and ginger	1 tbsp	1 tbsp	1 tbsp

Pound *jero*, with a little water, in a mortar to polish it. Pour into a large bowl, cover with water and thoroughly wash *jero*. Drain off water and put in fresh water, rinse the *jero* again and drain. Spread millet on a mat and dry in the sun, before grinding into a slightly coarse flour. Put water to boil in a large pot. Arrange a steamer inside the pot. Mix flour and spices with just enough water to bind it together. Mould *jero* flour into medium balls and arrange on the steamer in the pot. Cover pot and steam for 1½ hours. Take *fura* out and pound in a mortar into a smooth dough. Allow to cool and then mould to the size of a tennis ball. Sprinkle with *jero* flour saved to prevent *fura* sticking together. *Fura* will keep for a day or two before use.

FURA DA NONO

Nigeria

INGREDIENTS	Imperial	Metric	American
Per person:			
Small balls of ready-made fura	2	2	2
Sour milk	½ pint	250 ml	1¼ cups
or *Fresh milk mixed with natural yoghurt*	½ pint	250 ml	1¼ cups
Sugar or honey to taste			

In a large mixing bowl, put the milk and crush into it the *fura* until it is well mashed. Sweeten with sugar or honey. Serve in cereal bowls.

COUSCOUS DE SENEGALESE

Senegal

INGREDIENTS	Imperial	Metric	American
Beef or mutton, diced	2 lb	1 kg	2 lb
Ripe tomatoes	4	4	4
Medium carrots	4	4	4
Onion	1	1	1
Tin tomato purée, 5 oz/125 g	1	1	1
Medium turnips	2	2	2
Aubergine (eggplant)	1	1	1
Cauliflower	½	½	½
Cabbage	½	½	½
Small swede (rutabage)	1	1	1
Green beans	1 lb	450 g	1 lb
Parsley sprigs	2	2	2
Garlic clove, crushed	1	1	1
Cayenne pepper	1 tsp	1 tsp	1 tsp
Cooking oil	8 fl. oz	225 ml	1 cup
Lalu powder	1 tbsp	1 tbsp	1tbsp
Couscous granules			

Boil meat with salt, half the onion and garlic. Heat oil in the bottom pot of a *couscousier* (a three-piece cooking and steaming unit), and fry the rest of the onion, tomatoes, purée, pepper and a dash of salt. Cook for 15 minutes, stirring occasionally. Wash, clean and chop the rest of the vegetables and stir them into the sauce. Add the meat and the rest of the ingredients (except the *couscous*). Mix the *couscous* with some water, pour into the steamer and place over the sauce pot. Cook sauce and *couscous* for 40 minutes, take off *couscous* and sprinkle with some cold water and the *lalu* powder (made from the seed of the baobab) which helps *couscous* to soften more quickly and retain its granules. Pour back into the steamer and cover; reduce heat and steam 20 minutes more. Serve *couscous* hot with vegetable sauce and fried salted butter.

Steamed *couscous* makes an excellent gruel served with milk and sugar or honey.

Couscous granules are made either of wheat or millet. It is a laborious process. Fortunately it can be bought ready-made in kilo packs in the market.

KUNUN GEDA

 Nigeria

INGREDIENTS	Imperial	Metric	American
Raw groundnuts, puréed	1 lb	450 g	1 lb
Dawa-grain flour (barley-type millet)	8 oz	225 g	1 cup
Tsamia (souring pods)	4 oz	100 g	¼ lb
Sugar or honey to taste			

Soak the *tsamia* pods in ½ pint/250 ml/1¼ cups of water and put on one side. Thoroughly mix the groundnut purée with 2 pints/1.25 litres/5 cups of water and allow to settle. Pour the water into a deep cooking pot ensuring that the sediment does not go into the pot. Simmer on low heat for about one hour. Mix the *dawa* flour with water into a smooth paste. Stir this paste into the boiling water to make a thick pap. Stir in the sour liquid of the soaked *tsamia*. Serve in deep bowls or cereal bowls with sugar or honey to taste.

POISSON FARCI

 Senegal

INGREDIENTS	Imperial	Metric	American
Mullet	1	1	1
Garlic clove, crushed	1	1	1
Mixed spice	1 tbsp	1 tbsp	1 tbsp
Parsley	2 oz	50 g	
Spring or leaf onions	6	6	6
Tomatoes	2	2	2
Butter	1 tbsp	1 tbsp	1 tbsp
Salt			

Gently peel skin off whole from the fish and put aside. Bone the fish flesh and mash it, adding all the other ingredients. Pack mixture back into the fish skin and sew it with needle and thread. Gently pat back into shape. Brush the fish with butter and bake in an oven at low heat for 40 minutes. Serve in slices with fresh green salad.

THIEBOU DIENE

Senegal

INGREDIENTS	Imperial	Metric	American
Fresh fish	4 lb	2 kg	4 lb
Rice, washed and drained	1 lb	450 g	2½ cups
Ripe tomatoes, sliced	2 lb	1 kg	2 lb
Cauliflower	½ lb	225 g	½ lb
Cabbage	½ lb	225 g	½ lb
Lime juice	1 tbsp	1 tbsp	1 tbsp
Black pepper	1 tsp	1 tsp	1 tsp
Cayenne pepper	1 tsp	1 tsp	1 tsp
Tomato purée	4 tbsp	4 tbsp	4 tbsp
Turnips	2	2	2
Medium-sized aubergine (eggplant)	1	1	1
Parsley	1 oz	25 g	
Spring onions	4	4	4
Garlic clove, crushed	½	½	½
Groundnut oil	8 fl. oz	200 ml	1 cup
Salt to taste			

Cut the fish into cutlets and wash well, using the lime juice. Grind together the parsley, peppers, spring onion and garlic and mix well into the fish with salt. Leave fish to stand for a few minutes.

Wash and slice the vegetables. Heat oil in a deep saucepan and lightly fry the onion, add the tomatoes and tomato purée and stir. Put in the seasoned fish and the vegetables with a pint of water. Allow all to simmer for 30 minutes. Remove the fish and the vegetables from the sauce and leave in a covered dish. Stir the rice into the sauce adding more water if necessary. Reduce heat and cook rice until it is soft and all the liquid absorbed. Serve rice on a platter garnished with the fish and vegetables.

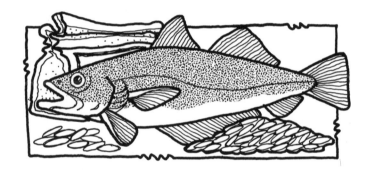

BREADFRUIT CHIPS

Seychelles

INGREDIENTS	Imperial	Metric	American
Firm ripe breadfruits	2	2	2
Salt to taste			
Oil to fry			

Peel and wash breadfruit. Slice and cut into fingers. Sprinkle with salt and fry until crisp and golden.

Serve hot as a side dish with meat curry.

YASSA

Senegal

INGREDIENTS	Imperial	Metric	American
Chicken, skinned	1	1	1
Large onions, sliced	4	4	4
Fresh limes or lemons	6	6	6
Black pepper	2 tsp	2 tsp	2 tsp
Cayenne pepper	1 tsp	1 tsp	1 tsp
Vinegar	1 tbsp	1 tbsp	1 tbsp
Groundnut oil	4 fl. oz	100 ml	½ cup
Salt to taste			

Cut chicken into portions and put in a large bowl. Add the onions, vinegar, juice of the limes, black pepper and cayenne. Mix all well with the chicken and leave to marinate for 30 minutes. Take the chicken out of the marinade and grill (broil) for 25 minutes. Heat oil in a saucepan and fry the chicken on low heat until golden brown, add the onion from the marinade and fry with the chicken. Add the rest of the marinade and a cup of water. Simmer for about 20 minutes. Serve with fluffy white rice.

BOUILLON DE POISSON

Seychelles

INGREDIENTS	Imperial	Metric	American
Fresh fish heads	4	4	4
Lemon	1	1	1
Peppercorns	½ tsp	½ tsp	½ tsp
Onion	1	1	1
Tomato purée	1 tbsp	1 tbsp	1 tbsp
Cooking oil	1 tbsp	1 tbsp	1 tbsp
Small well-rounded new potatoes	1 lb	450 g	1 lb
Mixed spices	½ tsp	½ tsp	½ tsp
Salt to taste			

Prepare a medium casserole. Wash and clean the fish heads and arrange in the casserole. Squeeze on them the juice of the fresh lemon. Sprinkle on salt and pepper. In a frying pan, melt the vegetable oil and fry the chopped onion. Pour it on the fish, add the tomato purée, the peppercorns, spices and the peeled potatoes. Cover the casserole and put in an oven 350 °F/180 °C/Gas Mark 4 for one hour, or until cooked and potatoes tender. Serve on its own or with fluffy white rice or boiled *yam*.

LA DAUB

Seychelles

INGREDIENTS	Imperial	Metric	American
Bananas or plantains	*4*	*4*	*4*
Yam	*2 lb*	*1 kg*	*2 lb*
Sweet potatoes	*2 lb*	*1 kg*	*2 lb*
Large coconuts	*2*	*2*	*2*
Cinnamon (cloves or vanilla may be substituted)	*2 tsp*	*2 tsp*	*2 tsp*
Sugar	*2 oz*	*50 g*	*¼ cup*

Peel *yam* and sweet potatoes, wash and put in a saucepan. Peel the bananas and put them in with the *yam*. Add the sugar.

Grate the coconuts and put in a bowl, add a pint of water and squeeze out the coconut milk thoroughly. Strain the milk and put in the saucepan with the *yam*, bananas and sweet potatoes. Add the cinnamon. Cover the saucepan and simmer on very low fire until *yam* is quite done and soft. Serve hot or cold as a dessert.

CURRY ZOURITE

Seychelles

INGREDIENTS	Imperial	Metric	American
Octopus	*6*	*6*	*6*
Lemon	*1*	*1*	*1*
Large onion, finely chopped	*1*	*1*	*1*
Fresh ginger, crushed	*2 tsp*	*2 tsp*	*2 tsp*
Tomato purée	*2 tbsp*	*2 tbsp*	*2 tbsp*
Fresh garlic, crushed	*1 tbsp*	*1 tbsp*	*1 tbsp*
Very hot Seychelles curry powder	*4 tbsp*	*4 tbsp*	*4 tbsp*
Beef stock cubes	*2*	*2*	*2*
Salt to taste			

With a wooden mallet, beat the octopus well, especially the tentacles, to tenderize them. Clean the octopus well and marinate for 1—2 hours in a mixture of lemon juice, salt, garlic and ginger.

In a saucepan, melt a knob (2 tbsp) of butter, fry the onion until tender, stir in the tomato purée, crush and stir in the chicken cube. Stir in the special Seychelles curry powder and the rest of the garlic and ginger. Add 1 pint/500 ml/2½ cups of water and simmer for 20 minutes, stirring occasionally. Add the marinated octopus and simmer until quite cooked. Serve hot with mixed fried rice.

Chin-Chin—page 79 and Puff-Puff—page 80

COCONUT RICE

Sierra Leone

INGREDIENTS	Imperial	Metric	American
Rice	1 lb	450 g	2½ cups
Large coconut	1	1	1
Large ripe tomatoes	4	4	4
Tomato purée	2 tbsp	2 tbsp	2 tbsp
Onion	1	1	1
Cayenne pepper	1 tsp	1 tsp	1 tsp
Cooking oil or coconut oil	6 fl. oz	150 ml	¾ cup
Butter	2 oz	50 g	¼ cup
Fresh prawns, shelled	4 oz	100 g	½ cup
Chicken portions	6	6	6
Salt to taste			

Wash and boil the chicken and prawns with salt, a pinch of thyme and a few sliced onions. When cooked, take out the chicken and prawns and fry them in heated oil in a frying pan. Add the coconut milk to the meat stock and then the rest of the ingredients, except the rice. Simmer for 20 minutes and gradually bring to the boil. Stir in the rice and cook until rice is soft and the moisture all absorbed. Serve on a platter garnished with the chicken and prawns.

To extract milk from a coconut, punch two holes in it and extract the juice. Then break coconut and shell, grate the flesh, put in a bowl and cover with water. With a squeezing, washing motion, wash the juice out of the coconut into the water. Strain off the milky water and add to the clear juice first drained off the coconut.

Coconut is eaten mainly as a snack on its own or with roasted sweet corn or boiled sliced *cassava*. The coconut oil for hairdressing is a very old African beauty product. Used in cooking it has a tantalizing aroma.

POISSON SALÉ

Seychelles

INGREDIENTS	Imperial	Metric	American
Dry fish	2 lb	1 kg	2 lb
Tomato purée	2 tbsp	2 tbsp	2 tbsp
Cooking oil	2 tbsp	2 tbsp	2 tbsp
Salt and pepper to taste			

Soak the dry fish for an hour, strip off the skin and crack it, breaking it into pieces. Flake into a dish, removing the bones. In a saucepan heat the oil and lightly fry the onion. Stir in the pepper and tomato, add the salt and simmer on a low fire for 20 minutes stirring constantly.

Add the fish and stir to work the fish into the sauce. Simmer for a further 15 minutes. Serve with rice or *yam*.

Ochra Soup—page 22
with Pounded Yam—page 14

JOLLOF RICE

Sierra Leone

INGREDIENTS	Imperial	Metric	American
Rice, washed and parboiled	2 lb	1 kg	2 lb
Ripe tomatoes, sliced	3 lb	1.35 kg	3 lb
Cans tomato purée (5 oz/125 g size)	4	4	4
Large onions, sliced	2	2	2
Cayenne pepper	3 tsp	3 tsp	3 tsp
Mixed spice and herbs	2 tsp	2 tsp	2 tsp
Butter	½ lb	225 g	1 cup
Chicken portions, beef or mutton	6	6	6
Black pepper	1 tsp	1 tsp	1 tsp
White pepper	1 tsp	1 tsp	1 tsp
Thyme	½ tsp	½ tsp	½ tsp
Salt to taste			
Cooking oil	8 fl. oz	200 ml	1 cup

Divide all ingredients into half, except rice, meat and oil. In a heavy pan, place all the meat and enough water to just cover it. Add half of the seasonings, and cook until tender. Heat all the oil in a skillet or heavy saucepan. Drain the meat and fry until brown before putting on one side. Lightly fry the tomatoes and onions in the same oil and add the reserved meat with the tomato purée. Collect the seasoning and continue to cook slowly for 25 minutes, stirring constantly.

Take a large saucepan and put the other half of the ingredients into it, with a pint of water and salt to taste. Gently bring to the boil and stir in the half-cooked rice. Reduce heat and cover pot. Simmer on very low heat until rice is cooked and all water and sauce absorbed. Cover pot and continue to heat slowly for about 30 minutes or longer. Serve hot, garnished with steamed cabbage and the stewed meat.

Jollof was originally a national dish of the Wolof-speaking tribes of Djolof, Cayor and Baol in Senegal. It is a special party dish enjoyed across West Africa, with variations of it in other parts of Africa.

ANAN GEIL

Somalia

INGREDIENTS	Imperial	Metric	American
Camel milk (anan geil)	1 pint	500 ml	2½ cups
Millet gruel	4 oz	100 g	¼ lb
Honey	2 fl. oz	50 ml	3 tbsp

Pour the milk into a mixing bowl and mash into it the millet gruel. Stir in the honey. Cover the bowl and chill slightly. Serve in cereal bowls.

FREJON

Sierra Leone

INGREDIENTS	Imperial	Metric	American
Black-eyed beans	1 lb	450 g	1 lb
Coconut	1	1	1
Sugar	2 tbsp	1 tbsp	2 tbsp
Mixed spice	1 tsp	1 tsp	1 tsp
Small bar plain (dark) chocolate **or** cocoa powder to colour	1	1	1

To skin beans: soak for 30 minutes and then drain off the water. Using both hands with a squeezing, washing action, peel the skins off the beans. Cover with water and the skins will float and can be collected in a sieve or strainer as the water is drained off into a second bowl. Repeat the sequence to skin the remaining beans.

After skinning, soak the beans. Extract coconut milk (page 00) and simmer beans in coconut milk. Add the sugar and cook beans until very soft. Allow to cool. Grind or liquidize the mixture and pour back into the saucepan. Melt the chocolate or cocoa powder in a cup of hot water. Stir into the bean purée with the spice and heat gently. Serve hot with fresh fish and *garri*.

Frejon is traditionally a Good Friday dish and eaten right across West Africa. There is no reason why this excellent dish should not be eaten at other times of the year.

BREES AND HILLIB STEW

Somalia

INGREDIENTS	Imperial	Metric	American
Brees *(rice)*	1 lb	450 g	4 cups
Hillib *(meat)*	2 lb	1 kg	2 lb
Ripe tomatoes, sliced	1 lb	450 g	1 lb
Large onion, sliced	1	1	1
Chilli powder	½ tsp	½ tsp	½ tsp
Butter or cooking oil	6 tbsp	6 tbsp	6 tbsp
Thyme	¼ tsp	¼ tsp	¼ tsp
Peppercorn	½ tsp	½ tsp	½ tsp
Salt to taste			

Wash and boil rice separately with salt. Cut the *hillib* into small pieces, wash and cook with salt, thyme, peppercorn and a few slices of onions, until soft and cooked. Lightly fry the meat in butter, add the onion and tomatoes and the meat stock and a little more water if need be. Simmer on a low fire for 40 minutes or until stew is done. Serve on the rice garnished with steamed cabbage.

MEALIE MEAL FRITTERS

 Swaziland

INGREDIENTS	Imperial	Metric	American
Cold mealie meal porridge	1 pint	500 ml	4 cups
Eggs	2	2	2
Flour	4 oz	100 g	1 cup
Oil to fry			
Caster sugar			

Mealie meal porridge can also be served hot with milk.

Porridge

	Imperial	Metric	American
Mealie meal	1 lb	450 g	1 lb
Sugar	4 oz	100 g	½ cup
Water	2 pints	1 litre	5 cups

Soak the meal for about 2 hours. Then bring the water to the boil in a cooking pot. Drain the grains from the water in which they have been soaking, put them into the boiling water and simmer over a low heat until the grains are soft and cooked. Stir in the sugar and allow to cool.

Beat together the mealie meal porridge and eggs, add sufficient flour to bind the mixture to a slightly soft, dropping consistency. Heat oil in a frying pan and fry the mixture by the tablespoonful, turning the fritters to brown both sides. Serve hot sprinkled with caster sugar.

MEALIE MEAL CAKES

 Swaziland

INGREDIENTS	Imperial	Metric	American
Mealie meal	6 oz	150 g	¾ cup
Flour	6 oz	150 g	1½ cups
Butter	6 oz	150 g	¾ cup
Sugar	6 oz	150 g	¾ cup
Baking powder	4 tsp	4 tsp	4 tsp
Salt	2 tsp	2 tsp	2 tsp
Egg	1	1	1
Milk	1 pint	500 ml	2½ cups

Combine the dry ingredients in a mixing bowl and rub in the butter. Beat the egg and add it to the mixture, pour in the milk and mix to a soft creamy dough. Spoon the mixture into shallow greased baking tins and bake for 25 minutes in pre-heated oven at 350 °F/180 °C/Gas Mark 4.

COCONUT DRINK

 Tanzania

Use large green coconuts.

Bore two holes in each coconut, extract the juice, pour into a jug and chill. Serve in wine glasses.

NDIZI NA NYAMA

 Tanzania

INGREDIENTS	Imperial	Metric	American
Cooking bananas or plantain, peeled and sliced	6	6	6
Mutton or beef	2 lb	1 kg	2 lb
Large onion, sliced	1	1	1
Ripe tomatoes	4	4	4
Tomato purée	1 tbsp	1 tbsp	1 tbsp
Coconut cream	2 tbsp	2 tbsp	2 tbsp
Mixed spice	1 tsp	1 tsp	1 tsp
White pepper	1 tsp	1 tsp	1 tsp
Salt to taste			

Cut meat into small pieces, wash, cover with water and cook in a saucepan with salt, seasoning and onions for 30 minutes. Remove the meat from the stock and put aside in a covered dish. Leave the stock on the cooker and add to it the tomatoes, coconut cream, pepper and a cup of water. Bring to the boil and add the banana slices. Cover pot and simmer for 20 minutes. Add the pre-cooked meat and continue to simmer a further 15 minutes. Serve hot.

CHICKEN PILAU

 Tanzania

INGREDIENTS	Imperial	Metric	American
Medium chicken, boned and diced	½	½	½
Brown rice	1 lb	450 g	2 cups
Tomato purée	1 tbsp	1 tbsp	1 tbsp
Fresh tomatoes, skinned and sliced	8 oz	225 g	½ lb
Medium onion, chopped	1	1	1
Butter	2 tbsp	2 tbsp	2 tbsp
Chilli powder	2 tsp	2 tsp	2 tsp
Mixed spice	2 tsp	2 tsp	2 tsp
Peas	2 oz	50 g	⅛ lb
Salt to taste			

Wash, drain and season the chicken with the mixed spices, salt and purée. Melt the butter in a saucepan and lightly fry the chicken and seasoning and onion. Add 1 pint of water, and simmer for 20 minutes.

Wash the rice, drain and stir into the chicken, add more water if necessary and cook over a very low fire until rice is cooked. Rinse and drain the peas and spread over the rice to steam for 10 minutes. Serve the rice hot garnished with the chicken.

CHACHANGA

 Togo

INGREDIENTS	Imperial	Metric	American
Mutton or beef	2 lb	1 kg	2 lb
Roasted groundnuts, ground	4 oz	100 g	¼ lb
Chilli powder	2 tsp	2 tsp	2 tsp
Groundnut oil	2 tbsp	2 tbsp	2 tbsp
Mixed spice	1 tbsp	1 tbsp	1 tbsp

Cut meat into pieces and slice thinly, rinse and allow to drain. Mix together the groundnut powder, chilli powder, spice and salt and pour onto a flat board. Thread the slices of meat onto skewers, press the skewers into the mixture on the board and thoroughly coat all sides of the meat. Sprinkle the meat with oil and grill very slowly for about 40 minutes, or roast over a barbecue.

This humble peasant snack has now become the aristocrat among delicacies at parties at all levels, everywhere in Africa. In Nigeria it is called *Tsire Agashe*, in Ghana it is called Chichinga and it has various other names elsewhere.

CHAKCHOUKA

 Tunisia

INGREDIENTS	Imperial	Metric	American
Medium sweet green peppers	4	4	4
Small firm ripe tomatoes	6	6	6
Small onions	2	2	2
Cooked shredded or ground meat	8 oz	225 g	½ lb
or Corned beef	8 oz	225 g	½ lb
Cloves garlic, ground	3	3	3
Butter	1 oz	25 g	⅛ cup
Black pepper	¼ tsp	¼ tsp	¼ tsp
Caraway seeds	½ tsp	½ tsp	½ tsp
Eggs, whisked (beaten)	2	2	2
Salt to taste			

Remove the seeds from the peppers. Slice all the vegetables and fry in the butter in a large frying pan until soft. Beat the eggs and stir into the frying pan, and continue cooking, stirring constantly. Stir in the shredded meat and cook for another 10 minutes. Add the rest of the ingredients and simmer for about 30 minutes. Serve hot with fresh baked rolls.

TAJINE

Tunisia

INGREDIENTS	Imperial	Metric	American
Black-eyed beans	1½ lb	750 g	1½ lb
Pieces of breast of chicken, boned	3	3	3
Onion, chopped	1	1	1
Tomato purée	2 tbsp	2 tbsp	2 tbsp
Spinach	½ lb	225 g	½ lb
Red sweet pepper, chopped	1	1	1
Green sweet pepper, chopped	1	1	1
Cheese, grated	4 oz	100 g	1 cup
Breadcrumbs	4 oz	100 g	1 cup
Eggs	6	6	6
Butter	4 oz	100 g	½ cup
Black pepper	1 tsp	1 tsp	1 tsp
Salt to taste			

Soak beans overnight. Wash the spinach thoroughly and parboil. Drain spinach, squeeze out surplus water and put aside. Cut the chicken into small pieces and season with salt and black pepper. Heat the butter in a saucepan and brown the chicken, adding the onion. Stir in the purée, peppers and beans, plus ⅝ pint/400 ml/2 cups of water. Allow to boil, lower the heat, cover the pot and simmer for about one hour. Reduce some of the sauce in a small pan.

To the beans add the breadcrumbs, cheese, spinach and more butter and salt if necessary. Stir in the eggs. Pour the *tajine* into a greased roasting tin and bake in a moderate oven until all moisture is absorbed and the *tajine* is firm. Cut into slices and serve hot with the reserved sauce.

CREOLE SHRIMPS

Togo

INGREDIENTS	Imperial	Metric	American
Fresh shrimps	2 lb	1 kg	2 lb
Medium onion, chopped	1	1	1
Celery stick, chopped	1	1	1
Garlic clove, crushed	1	1	1
Green pepper, sliced	1	1	1
Cayenne pepper	½ tsp	½ tsp	½ tsp
Cooking oil	2 tbsp	2 tbsp	2 tbsp
Tomato purée	2 tbsp	2 tbsp	2 tbsp
Rice, cooked	8 tbsp	8 tbsp	8 tbsp
Basil	½ tsp	½ tsp	½ tsp
Salt to taste			

Clean and wash shrimps and drain well. Heat oil in a saucepan and fry the shrimps. Add the garlic, stir in the onion and fry for five minutes. Stir in the rest of the ingredients and 4 fl. oz/400 ml/½ cup of water. Cover pot and simmer for 30 minutes. Serve hot in bowls topped with grated cheese.

DOULMA

Tunisia

INGREDIENTS	Imperial	Metric	American
Mutton, minced (ground)	1 lb	450 g	1 lb
Mutton, diced	1 lb	450 g	1 lb
Chopped parsley	1 tbsp	1 tbsp	1 tbsp
Small onion, minced	1	1	1
Eggs	2	2	2
Marrows (zucchini)	2	2	2
Black pepper	1 tsp	1 tsp	1 tsp
Cooking oil	1 tbsp	1 tbsp	1 tbsp
Tomato purée	1 tbsp	1 tbsp	1 tbsp
Black-eyed beans, soaked overnight	1 lb	450 g	2 cups
Lemon juice	1 tsp	1 tsp	1 tsp
Salt to taste			

Peel marrows and cut crosswise, cleaning out the insides. Fill each piece of marrow with a mixture of the minced mutton, onion and eggs. Put them aside. Season the diced mutton with salt and pepper and fry in a saucepan. Stir in the tomato purée and the washed and drained beans. Add 16 fl. oz/100 g/2 cups of water and simmer over a low heat for about an hour. Place the stuffed marrows in the saucepan with the beans, cover pot and continue to simmer for 30 minutes more. Pour on a little melted butter. Serve hot.

MARKIT OMMALAH

Tunisia

INGREDIENTS	Imperial	Metric	American
Veal, diced	1 lb	450 g	1 lb
Medium onion, finely chopped	1	1	1
Chilli powder	1 tsp	1 tsp	1 tsp
Black pepper	¼ tsp	¼ tsp	¼ tsp
Coriander	¼ tsp	¼ tsp	¼ tsp
Tomato purée	2 tbsp	2 tbsp	2 tbsp
Black-eyed beans	8 oz	225 g	½ lb
Olive	4 fl. oz	100 ml	½ cup
Vinegar	2 tbsp	2 tbsp	2 tbsp
Cooking oil	2 tbsp	2 tbsp	2 tbsp

Soak beans overnight. Rinse meat, drain, season with salt, black pepper, coriander and fry in the oil until soft. Add the onion and lightly fry. Stir in the cleaned beans and the rest of the ingredients, except the vinegar and olives. Cook beans until it is done and soft. Stir in the vinegar and olives. Serve hot.

EGGS AND MEAT BALL AJJA

 Tunisia

INGREDIENTS	Imperial	Metric	American
Mutton, minced (ground)	1 lb	450 g	1 lb
Dry mint leaves, ground	1 tbsp	1 tbsp	1 tbsp
Tomato purée	1 tbsp	1 tbsp	1 tbsp
Eggs	4	4	4
Water	8 fl. oz	200 ml	1 cup
Crushed garlic	1 tsp	1 tsp	1 tsp
Mixed coriander and ground cloves	1 tsp	1 tsp	1 tsp
Black pepper	½ tsp	½ tsp	½ tsp
Tabil (mixed spices)	1 tsp	1 tsp	1 tsp
Cooking oil	6 tbsp	6 tbsp	6 tbsp
Green sweet pepper, sliced	½	½	½
Red pepper, sliced	½	½	½
Caraway seed, ground	½ tsp	½ tsp	½ tsp
Salt to taste			

Combine minced mutton, salt, *tabil*, black pepper and ground mint; mix and mould into small balls and deep fry in hot oil over a low heat until cooked and brown. Take out meat balls and put aside in a pan. Add to the hot oil the tomato purée, peppers, garlic, caraway seed and a glass of water. Simmer for 20 minutes. Add the fried meat balls, stir the eggs into the sauce and simmer for 15 minutes more. Serve with fluffy cooked rice or freshly baked bread.

Other types of *ajja* are prepared using herrings or brains.

SWEET COUSCOUS

 Tunisia

INGREDIENTS	Imperial	Metric	American
Couscous	8 oz	225 g	½ lb
Water	6 tbsp	6 tbsp	6 tbsp
Olive oil	2 tbsp	2 tbsp	2 tbsp
Raisins	4 oz	100 g	1 cup
Butter	1 oz	25 g	⅛ cup
Sugar	2 tbsp	2 tbsp	2 tbsp

Moisten *couscous* with water and olive oil and mix well. Bring to steaming point in a *couscoussier* and cook for 15 minutes after it starts to steam. Pour *couscous* into a bowl and break up any lumps, sprinkle with water and return to the *couscoussier* to steam another 15 minutes. Repeat the process twice more or until *couscous* is soft and tender. Stir in the raisins, sugar and butter and steam a further 10 minutes. Pour into a dish and serve in small bowls with hot milk.

SAMSA

Tunisia

INGREDIENTS	Imperial	Metric	American
Almonds, blanched	*1 lb*	*450 g*	*1 lb*
Orange peel, grated	*2 tsp*	*2 tsp*	*2 tsp*
Caster sugar	*4 oz*	*100 g*	*½ cup*
Geranium water	*1 tbsp*	*1 tbsp*	*1 tbsp*
Lemon or lime juice	*2 tsp*	*2 tsp*	*2 tsp*
Roasted sesame seeds	*1 oz*	*25 g*	*¼ cup*

Crush the almonds in a mortar, mix in two-thirds of the sugar and the orange peel. In a saucepan bring to boil 8 fl. oz/200 ml/1 cup of water, add the rest of the sugar and the lemon juice to make a syrup, stir constantly. Add the geranium water, remove from heat and allow to cool.

Cut sheets of *malsouqua* into halves diagonally and place a small portion of almond mixture in each triangle. Fold the *malsouqua* around the almond stuffing several times. Fry the triangles in very hot oil until crisp and brown. Drain on absorbent paper and then soak the samsas in the syrup for 5 minutes. Coat each with sesame seeds and store.

Malsouqua are very thin sheets of pastry made from semolina. A useful substitute is the Greek 'phyllo' pastry which can be bought ready-made from Greek pastrycooks.

JANJALO MUCHUZI

Uganda

INGREDIENTS	Imperial	Metric	American
Red kidney beans	*1 lb*	*450 g*	*1 lb*
Onions, chopped	*2*	*2*	*2*
Large ripe tomatoes, chopped	*3*	*3*	*3*
Tomato purée	*2 tbsp*	*2 tbsp*	*2 tbsp*
Chilli powder	*2 tsp*	*2 tsp*	*2 tsp*
Mixed spice	*1 tsp*	*1 tp*	*1 tsp*
Fresh fish	*2 lb*	*1 kg*	*2 lb*
Salt to taste			

Soak kidney beans overnight, drain off water and rinse through in a colander, then boil in salt water for about 45 minutes. Add the rest of the ingredients except the fish and simmer for 30 minutes. Add the fish and continue to simmer for 20 minutes more. Serve warm.

MATOKE N'YAMA

 Uganda

INGREDIENTS	Imperial	Metric	American
Green plantains (matoke)	4	4	4
Onions, chopped	2	2	2
Fresh tomatoes, chopped	3	3	3
Tomato purée	1 tbsp	1 tbsp	1 tbsp
Cooking oil	4 tbsp	4 tbsp	4 tbsp
Chilli powder	1 tsp	1 tsp	1 tsp
Mixed spice	1 tsp	1 tsp	1 tsp
Meat (n'yama)	2 lb	1 kg	2 lb

Boil the meat with salt and some of the onion. Peel and slice the plantains and soak in cold water. Heat oil in a saucepan and fry the onion, tomatoes, chilli, tomato purée and spice. Add the boiled meat and its stock and bring to the boil. Add the plantains with 16 fl. oz/400 ml/2 cups of water. Cover pot and simmer over a low heat until the plantains are cooked. Serve hot.

You may prefer *Matoke Ngege* (fish), in which case the fish should be added at the very end, after the plantains.

Mogo (cassava) is another staple diet of Uganda and is prepared in the same way as *matoke*.

POLENTA PIE

 Zambia

INGREDIENTS	Imperial	Metric	American
Maize flour (cornmeal)	1 lb	450 g	3 cups
Shredded (ground meat) (or chicken)	8 oz	225 g	1 cup
Margarine	2 oz	50 g	¼ cup
Milk	1½ pints	750 ml	3¼ cups
Peppercorn	1 tsp	1 tsp	1 tsp
Coriander			
Dash thyme			
Salt & pepper to taste			
Cube meat stock	1	1	1

Set the oven at 350 °F/180 °C/Gas Mark 4. Heat 1 pint/500 ml/2½ cups of the milk and the margarine, and bring to the boil. Mix the maize flour with the rest of the milk into a smooth paste. Stir paste into the boiling milk to make a thick slightly stiff dough.

Line the inside of a well-greased oven dish with two-thirds of the dough. Mix the shredded meat with the crushed meat cube, pepper, salt and seasonings. Arrange in the pie dish.

Roll out the rest of the dough and cover the pie with it, trimming and decorating the edges with bits of dough. Bake the pie in the pre-heated oven for about one hour. Serve hot with peas or beans.

SOSATIES

Zimbabwe

INGREDIENTS	Imperial	Metric	American
Mutton	2 lb	1 kg	2 lb
Curry powder	1 tbsp	1 tbsp	1 tbsp
Large red pepper	1	1	1
Green pepper	1	1	1
Chilli powder	1 tsp	1 tsp	1 tsp
Onion, sliced	1 lb	450 g	1 lb
Tamarind, chopped	2 oz	50 g	2 oz
Bay leaves	2	2	2
Cooking oil	3 tbsp	3 tbsp	3 tbsp

Thinly slice the onion and lightly fry in a little oil. Take off the heat. Add the curry, chilli powder, bay leaves and tamarind juice. Dice the meat and work into the mixture. Leave for 8 hours or overnight. Weave the pieces of mutton onto small skewers and fry in a saucepan until brown and cooked. Add the mixture and simmer for 30 minutes. Serve hot with mashed potatoes.

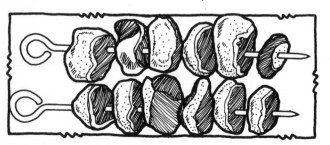

SWEET POTATO COOKIES

Zimbabwe

INGREDIENTS	Imperial	Metric	American
Grated raw sweet potatoes	1 lb	450 g	1 lb
Honey	4 fl. oz	100 ml	½ cup
Lemon rind, grated	1 tsp	1 tsp	1 tsp
Butter	4 oz	100 g	½ cup
Sugar	4 oz	100 g	½ cup
Egg	1	1	1
Salt	½ tsp	½ tsp	½ tsp
Milk	6 tbsp	6 tbsp	6 tbsp
Flour, sifted	½ lb	450 g	2 cups
Baking powder	1 tsp	1 tsp	1 tsp

Cream sugar and butter together in a mixing bowl. Blend in the egg, honey, lemon rind and sweet potatoes. Blend into the mixture the flour, baking powder and salt. With a teaspoon, put small bits of mixture 2 in./5 cm apart on a greased baking tray. With a toothpick, prick holes on each cookie.

Bake for 20 minutes in a hot oven 350 °F/180 °C/Gas Mark 4 or until cookies are cooked and golden. Take tray out of oven and allow to cool for about 5 minutes before removing cookies.

Korokoro—page 80

Chapter Five

SWEET, DRINKS, AND SERVING IDEAS

NIGER PINEAPPLE

INGREDIENTS	Imperial	Metric	American
Medium pineapple (or canned pineapple)	1	1	1
Large tin condensed milk	1	1	1
Gelatine	2 tsp	2 tsp	2 tsp
Pineapple juice	8 fl. oz	200 ml	1 cup

Dissolve gelatine in a little boiling water and mix in the milk and pineapple juice. Allow to cool. Peel and cut pineapple into pieces and then crush it and whisk it into the gelatine mixture until the mixture thickens. Pour into small waxed paper cases or other small containers and allow to set for about one hour.

Curried Meat Triangles—page 28

MANGO SLICE

Rich shortcrust pastry	Imperial	Metric	American
Flour	4 oz	100 g	1 cup
Caster sugar	2 tbsp	2 tbsp	2 tbsp
Salt	½ tsp	½ tsp	½ tsp
Egg yolk	1	1	1
Lemon juice	1 tbsp	1 tbsp	1 tbsp
Butter, soft but not melted	6 tbsp	6 tbsp	6 tbsp

Combine flour, sugar and salt in a mixing bowl. Make a 'well' in the centre of the flour and put in the egg yolk and lemon juice. Mix the flour into them by degrees. When they have been taken up by the flour, gradually work in the butter until the mixture clings together, leaving the sides of the bowl. Cover and leave in a cold place for 30 minutes before rolling out.

Filling	Imperial	Metric	American
Thick custard	18 fl. oz	450 ml	2¼ cups
Vanilla extract	½ tsp	½ tsp	½ tsp
Large ripe mangoes, sliced	2	2	2
Small packet fruit jelly (gelatine)	1	1	1
Vanilla Custard	Imperial	Metric	American
Eggs	4	4	4
or Egg yolks	6—8	6—8	6—8
Milk	1 pint	500 ml	2½ cups
Sugar	4 oz	100 g	½ cup
Salt	¼ tsp	¼ tsp	¼ tsp
Vanilla extract **or** Vanilla bean	1½ tsp	1½ tsp	1½ tsp

To make custard: beat eggs or yolks with sugar and salt. Bring milk to boiling point and stir quickly into eggs. Cook the mixture over hot water, stirring constantly until it thickens, being careful not to overcook it. Take it off the heat source as soon as it begins to thicken and cool it before use. To flavour it either add vanilla extract at this point or put a vanilla bean into the milk while it is heating. It must be taken out before the milk is added to the eggs, but it can be washed and dried for later use.

Line a well greased oven-proof dish with the pastry and bake 'blind' in a hot oven. 400 °F/200 °C/ Gas Mark 6 for about 20 minutes. Mix the vanilla essence into the custard and spread over the cooled pastry. Arrange the peeled sliced mangoes over the custard. Dissolve jelly in half a pint of boiling water and allow to cool. Spoon jelly over mangoes and leave to set. Serve cut in slices.

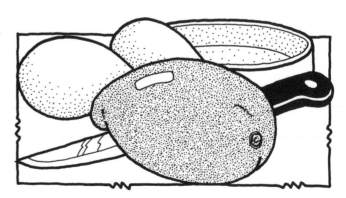

BANANA ICE CREAM

INGREDIENTS	Imperial	Metric	American
Bananas, mashed	4	4	4
Vanilla custard	½ pint	250 ml	1¼ cups
Sugar	8 oz	225 g	1 cup
Cream, whipped	½ pint	250 ml	1¼ cups
Sliced banana to decorate	1	1	1
Cochineal (red food colouring)			
Vanilla Custard			
Eggs	2	2	2
or Egg yolks	3—4	3—4	3—4
Milk	½ pint	250 ml	1¼ cups
Sugar	2 oz	50 g	¼ cup
Salt	⅛ tsp	⅛ tsp	⅛ tsp
Vanilla extract	1 tsp	1 tsp	1 tsp
or Vanilla bean			

Vanilla Custard Method: beat eggs or egg yolks with sugar and salt. Bring milk to boiling point and stir quickly into eggs. Cook the egg and milk mixture over hot water, in a double boiler or a bain-marie, stirring constantly until the custard thickens. Do not over-cook it; take it off the heat source as soon as it begins to thicken and cool it before use. To flavour it, either put a vanilla bean into the milk while it is heating (take it out before mixing milk and eggs; it can be washed and dried for later use) or add vanilla extract, ½—1 teaspoonful, after taking the custard from the heat.

Ice cream:
Mix mashed banana with the custard and sugar, fold in the whipped cream and add a few drops of cochineal. Freeze and serve decorated with the sliced banana.

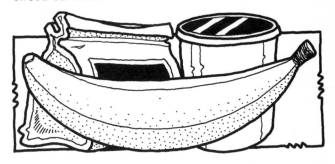

PAWPAW PLAIN

The pawpaw is a delicious fruit, with flesh like a very juicy peach. Many Europeans and Americans will have only seen it as an ingredient of ice cream or served like a melon, with sugar. Try this way of serving, which brings out its flavour.

Peel and slice 2 medium ripe pawpaw lengthwise. Arrange in a bowl and sprinkle with a dash of salt. Chill slightly before serving.

PAWPAW FOOL

INGREDIENTS	Imperial	Metric	American
Medium pawpaw (not over-ripe)	1	1	1
Caster sugar	4 tbsp	4 tbsp	4 tbsp
Vanilla custard (cold)	16 fl. oz	400 ml	2 cups
Whipped cream or ice cream			

Custard:

Eggs	3	3	3
or Egg yolks	4—6	4—6	4—6
Milk	¾ pint	375 ml	1⅞ cups
Sugar	3 oz	75 g	⅜ cup
Salt	¼ tsp	¼ tsp	¼ tsp
Vanilla extract	1 tsp	1 tsp	1 tsp
or Vanilla bean			

Custard method: beat eggs or egg yolks with sugar and salt. Bring milk to boiling point and stir quickly into eggs. Cook the egg and milk mixture over hot water, in a double boiler or bain-marie, stirring constantly until the custard thickens. Do not over-cook; take it off the heat source as soon as it begins to thicken and cool it before use. To flavour it, either put a vanilla bean into the milk while it is heating (take it out before mixing the milk and eggs; it can be washed and dried for later use) or add vanilla extract after taking the custard from the heat.

To make the fool:

Peel pawpaw and cut into chunks. Place in a saucepan with 8 fl. oz/200 ml/1 cup of water and bring to the boil. Reduce the heat and simmer for 10 minutes. Turn into a bowl, add the sugar and mash the pawpaw. Stir in the custard and allow to cool slightly. Spoon into individual serving glasses and leave to cool, covered with a sheet of cling film. Just before serving, top each glass with whipped cream or ice cream.

AFRICAN FRUIT BOWL

INGREDIENTS	Imperial	Metric	American
Large pineapple	1	1	1
Assorted fresh fruit, diced			
Whipped cream or two small blocks of ice cream			

The two halves of the pineapple, scooped out, provide the 'bowls' for this dish.

Cut pineapple in half, scoop out the flesh and chop it into dice. Mix with diced fruits and pile them back into the pineapple shells, pouring the fruit juices over. Top with whipped cream or ice cream.

FRUITY PUNCH

INGREDIENTS	Imperial	Metric	American
Oranges	6	6	6
Pineapple, diced	½	½	½
Pawpaw, diced	½	½	½
Guavas, diced	2	2	2
Can pineapple juice	1	1	1
Lemonade	1 pint	500 ml	2½ cups

Squeeze the oranges and add the juice to the rest of the ingredients. Whisk in the lemonade and serve in tall glasses.

ICY ORANGE SHAKE

INGREDIENTS	Imperial	Metric	American
Juice of oranges	3	3	3
or Orange squash	1 pint	500 ml	2½ cups
Milk	1 pint	500 ml	2½ cups
Ice cream, small bar	1	1	1

Put all the ingredients in a mixing bowl and whisk well or blend in a blender for three minutes. Pour into a jug and chill. Serve in tall glasses topped with cubes of orange flesh.

GINGER ALE

INGREDIENTS

	Imperial	Metric	American
Fresh ginger, peeled	*2 lb*	*1 kg*	*2 lb*
Sugar to taste			

Wash ginger and crush in a mortar or mince it. Put it in a deep saucepan, add the sugar and cover with the water. Simmer over very low heat for about three hours, when most of the water will have evaporated. Allow to cool. Pour into a jug and serve chilled.

CHINANADZI
(PINEAPPLE DRINK)

INGREDIENTS

	Imperial	Metric	American
Large ripe pineapple	*1*	*1*	*1*
Boiling water	*2 pints*	*1.25 litres*	*5 cups*
Ground ginger	*1 tsp*	*1 tsp*	*1 tsp*
Ground cloves	*1 tsp*	*1 tsp*	*1 tsp*
Sugar	*1 oz*	*25 g*	*⅛ cup*

Peel and slice pineapple and put in a bowl. Add the spice and sugar and pour on it the boiling water. Cover bowl and allow to cool overnight. Strain the drink and serve on ice in tall glasses.

Chapter Six

SNACKS

CHIN-CHIN

INGREDIENTS	Imperial	Metric	American
Self-raising flour or flour sifted with 4 tsp baking powder	1 lb	450 g	4 cups
Caster sugar	4 oz	100 g	½ cup
Grated nutmeg	½ tsp	½ tsp	½ tsp
Eggs	3	3	3
Knob of margarine			
Oil to fry			

Sift the flour and rub in enough margarine to soften the pastry. Whisk (beat) the eggs and sugar together, and beat in the nutmeg. Fold in the flour and knead into a smooth but stiff dough. Turn the dough onto a floured board, and roll out thinly. Divide into three or four portions for easier handling. Roll out each portion thinly, cut into ribbons about 1 in./2.5 cm wide, and further cut the ribbons diagonally into pieces. Pierce the centre of each piece, lift up the piece and pull one end of it through the centre cut to make it look like a bow. Place the pastry bows on a floured tray. Continue the process until the pastry is used up. Heat some groundnut oil in a frying pan and fry the *chin-chin* in small batches on a low heat until golden brown on both sides. Allow *chin-chin* to cool then serve cold or store in a biscuit tin.

PUFF-PUFF

INGREDIENTS	Imperial	Metric	American
Self-raising flour or flour sifted with 4 tsp baking powder	1 lb	450 g	4 cups
Caster sugar	4 tbsp	4 tbsp	4 tbsp
Eggs	3	3	3
Knob of butter	1	1	1 tbsp
Drops vanilla extract	2	2	2
Sultanas and raisins (optional)	1 oz	25 g	¼ cup
Oil to fry			

Sift flour and rub into it the knob of butter. Beat together the eggs, sugar, essence and dry fruits and fold in the flour. Mix well into a smooth dropping consistency, but not watery. Scoop up a little at a time in the hollow of your fingers and deep-fry in hot oil on a moderate heat. Fry up to eight puff-puffs at a time. Serve hot or cold.

KOROKORO

INGREDIENTS	Imperial	Metric	American
Coarse corn meal flour	8 oz	225 g	1 cup
Sugar	2 tbsp	2 tbsp	2 tbsp
Oil to fry			

Mix flour and sugar with sufficient hot water to make a soft but stiff dough. Leave aside for 20 minutes to settle and cool. Take a bit at a time and roll with your flat palm into a long pencil-slim sticks. Connect the ends of some of them to form rings. Fry in hot oil until golden brown.

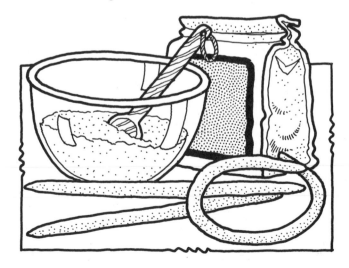

GROUNDNUT COOKIES

INGREDIENTS	Imperial	Metric	American
Roasted groundnuts	1 lb	450 g	8 cups
Sugar	2 tbsp	2 tbsp	2 tbsp
Lime or lemon juice	1 tbsp	1 tbsp	1 tbsp
Water	8 fl. oz	200 ml	1 cup

Dissolve sugar in water in a saucepan and bring to the boil. Reduce heat and when the water becomes slightly sticky, stir in the groundnuts and lime juice, stirring continuously until quite sticky. Pour into a buttered sandwich (cake) tin and spread evenly with a spatula. Mark into squares with the point of a knife, allow to cool and cut into squares.

YAM BALLS

INGREDIENTS	Imperial	Metric	American
Yam, boiled	2 lb	1 kg	2 lb
Eggs, beaten	3	3	3
Corned beef	1 oz	25 g	⅛ cup
Oil to deep fry			

Mash cooked yam with one beaten egg. Mix crushed corned beef into the two beaten eggs, with a pinch of salt. Mould mashed yam into small balls, dip each into the egg mixture and deep fry in hot oil until golden brown. Serve hot, alone or with hot peas or baked beans.

Yam balls are a favourite with West Africans, especially at church bazaars. They make a lovely addition to a buffet.

Sometimes, slices of tomatoes, onions and red sweet peppers are mixed with the mashed yam before it is moulded into balls.

KOSAI-AKARA

INGREDIENTS	Imperial	Metric	American
Black-eyed beans	8 oz	225 g	½ lb
Large onion, finely chopped	1	1	1
Chilli powder	1 tsp	1 tsp	1 tsp
Egg (optional)	1	1	1
Salt to taste			
Oil to deep fry			

Clean and liquidize or grind soaked beans. Stir in the onion, salt and pepper and beat in the egg with a wooden spoon. Deep fry spoonsfuls, up to eight at a time. Halfway through frying, turn *kosai* to fry the other sides. Serve hot with *agidi* (page 83) or freshly baked bread. The mixture will look more attractive if the beans are skinned before grinding.

To skin beans:

Soak for 30 minutes and then drain off the water. Using both hands with a squeezing, washing action, peel the skins off the beans. Cover with water and the skins will float and can be collected in a sieve or strainer as the water is drained off into a second bowl. Repeat the sequence to skin the remaining beans.

Akara can be fried in either groundnut oil or palmnut oil. There are a variety of *akara* and the Yozuba of Western Nigeria usually eat some with their morning corn or millet hot pap.

KULI-KULI

INGREDIENTS	Imperial	Metric	American
Roasted groundnuts	2 lb	1 kg	2 lb
Warm water	4 fl. oz	100 ml	½ cup
Groundnut oil to deep fry			

Clean groundnuts and grind or liquidize. Mould into a ball and with a kneading squeezing action, extract as much oil from them as possible, adding a little warm water from time to time to coax the oil out. Shape what is left into small flat or round biscuits and deep fry in their own oil, adding extra cooking oil if necessary.

Kuli-Kuli, the favourite of African children everywhere, provides a coating for roasting meat and mixes well with *lansur* salad (page 51).

DANKALI DA GEDA

INGREDIENTS	Imperial	Metric	American
Sweet potatoes (dankali)	2 lb	1 kg	2 lb
Roasted groundnuts (geda)	½ lb	225 g	4 cups

Boil *dankali* with salt but do not peel. When cooked allow to cool and serve with roasted groundnuts. Pepper sauce (page 26) and fried eggs can be served instead of groundnuts.

Rogo or *Mogo* (*cassava*) can be cooked and served as for *dankali*.

COCONUT AND SWEET CORN

INGREDIENTS	Imperial	Metric	American
Small corn on the cob	6	6	6
or large tin of sweetcorn	1	1	1
Coconut	1	1	1

Boil corn in a deep saucepan until cooked, then add a dash of salt. If canned corn is used, heat with a knob of butter. Shell the coconut and wash clean. Slice very thinly and serve with the corn.

Corn is one of Africa's staple foods; ground or liquidized into a paste, it is made into *pap* (like custard). A thick *pap* moulded in large wrapping leaves and allowed to cool is called *agidi* in some parts and is served with soups or stews. Ground into flour, the corn provides us with a stiff hot pudding called *fufu*. Corn can be boiled or roasted or made into popcorn. *Agidi* is delicious mashed into milk and sugar.

OJOJO

INGREDIENTS	Imperial	Metric	American
Fresh water-yam	*2 lb*	*1 kg*	*2 lb*
Chilli powder	*1 tsp*	*1 tsp*	*1 tsp*
Small onion, finely chopped	*1*	*1*	*1*
Salt to taste			
Oil to deep fry			

Peel, wash and grate *yam*. Beat in salt, pepper and onion. Deep fry in hot oil. If the grated *yam* is too watery, mix in a small amount of ground rice to thicken it.

Water-yam is so called because of the large quantity of moisture in this tuberous root. It is better suited than ordinary *yam* to dishes where grated *yam* is essential.

DODO AND GROUNDNUTS

INGREDIENTS	Imperial	Metric	American
Plantains	*3*	*3*	*3*
Pinch of ground ginger to mix in oil (optional)			
Salt to taste			
Oil to fry			
Roasted salted groundnuts	*8 oz*	*225 g*	*4 cups*

Peel plantains and slice diagonally. Sprinkle with salt and fry in shallow oil (adding ginger to oil, if desired). Turn to fry both sides until light golden brown. Serve with groundnuts or pepper sauce (see page 00).

Plantain is one of Africa's most versatile foods. Small plantains are a species without the centre 'seed cord'. These are preboiled, drained and dried in the sun. They are then stored away and eaten like biscuits. The large plantains are usually fried and eaten with pepper sauce (page 26) or served as a garnish with rice. It is served with groundnuts by women who sell from their large frying pans set up in the streets of Accra.

Plantain can be added to yams or beans and cooked in a rich tomato and pepper sauce.

Wine made from plantains is a speciality of the Cameroon.

DUNDU

INGREDIENTS	Imperial	Metric	American
Yam *or sweet potatoes*	2 lb	1 kg	2 lb
Salt to taste			
Oil to deep fry			

Peel, slice or chip *yam* or sweet potatoes, wash, drain and salt. Deep fry in hot oil until cooked. Serve hot with omelette or pepper sauce (page 00).

Either groundnut oil or palmnut oil can be used to fry the *yam*. A mixture of chilli powder and salt is served in a side dish to eat with it if preferred to pepper sauce or omelette.

Dundu is a simple enough dish but can be turned into an even more delicious dish by first cooking the slices of *yam*. Dip each slice in beaten egg before frying.

Yams come in season; newly harvested *yam* is very moist and is easily boiled or fried. Last year's harvest is very dry and has little moisture but very tasty. To fry the 'dry' *yam*, either add water to the oil so that the *yam* is boiled-fried in one operation or first boil the *yam* before frying.

GUGURU DA GEDA

INGREDIENTS	Imperial	Metric	American
Popping corn	4 oz	100 g	½ cup
Groundnuts, roasted	4 oz	100 g	2 cups
Salt	1 tsp	1 tsp	1 tsp
Cooking oil	1 tbsp	1 tbsp	1 tbsp

Pour oil into a deep saucepan and sprinkle with salt. Spread corn to cover base of saucepan and cover pot. Put on a very low fire. The corn should soon start to pop, do not open pot until the popping has stopped. Serve warm or cold with groundnuts.

SWEET GUGURU

Pour the oil in a deep saucepan. Spread the corn to cover base of saucepan and cover pot. The corn soon starts popping. Do not take the lid off pot until the popping has stopped. Then remove lid and sprinkle the popped corn with sugar. Toss it to spread the sugar. Serve hot or cold.

ROASTED SALTED GROUNDNUTS

INGREDIENTS	Imperial	Metric	American
Raw shelled groundnuts	2 lb	1 kg	2 lb
Salt	1 tbsp	1 tbsp	1 tbsp

Soak groundnuts in hot salted water for one hour and then drain. Spread the groundnuts on a baking sheet or tray and put under a hot grill (broiler). Turn them over from time to time with a spatula to ensure they are evenly roasted and cook until crisp. Test by crushing the skin off one or two to see if they are done. Cool and store in a jar.

IPEKERE

INGREDIENTS	Imperial	Metric	American
Half-ripe plantains	2	2	2
Salt to taste			
Palmnut oil to deep fry			

Peel plantains and cut in half. Slice lengthwise and sprinkle with salt. Leave on one side for five minutes. Heat palmnut oil and deep fry plantains until crisp. Serve hot or cold.

BANANA FRITTERS

INGREDIENTS	Imperial	Metric	American
Bananas, cut into small chunks	6	6	6
Sugar	2 tbsp	2 tbsp	2 tbsp
Plain flour	4 oz	100 g	1 cup
Egg white	1	1	1
Pinch of salt			
Oil to deep fry			

Make the batter by sifting the flour and salt into a bowl with a tablespoon of cooking oil and a small amount of water. Mix well. Add more water and beat to a coating consistency. Whisk (whip) the egg white until stiff and fold into the batter. Use immediately. Dip each chunk of banana into the batter using a long pointed stick or fork, hold over the bowl for a few seconds to allow excess batter to drain off, and deep fry until crisp and golden. Drain on absorbent paper. Serve hot, sprinkled with sugar.

Pineapple fritters can be made by the same method.

KAKRO

INGREDIENTS	Imperial	Metric	American
Coarse corn meal flour	8 oz	225 g	1 cup
Over-ripe bananas	6	6	6
Ginger powder	1 tsp	1 tsp	1 tsp
Coconut oil (or any cooking oil) to deep fry			

Mash bananas and fold in the corn meal flour. Mix in some warm water to make a slightly dropping consistency, and allow to settle for a few minutes. Heat oil and add the ginger powder to it. Deep fry small scoops of mixture, frying up to eight at a time. Serve hot or cold.

SUGARCANE WHEELS

INGREDIENTS	Imperial	Metric	American
Piece of sugar cane	12 in.	30 cm	12 in.

Scrape outer skin of sugar cane until cane is quite clean. Cut cane into ½ in./1.25 cm wheels with a sharp knife. Serve daintily arranged on a flat dish.

COCONUT CANDY

INGREDIENTS	Imperial	Metric	American
Coconut, shelled	1	1	1
Lime	1	1	1
Sugar	4 oz	100 g	½ cup
Water	6 fl. oz	175 ml	½ cup

Slice coconut very thinly and dice each slice into tiny rice-sized pieces. Heat the water and sugar and bring to the boil. Squeeze in two teaspoons of lime juice. When it starts to get syrupy, stir in the coconut and reduce the heat. Continue to stir until candy is quite sticky. Turn into a greased dish and allow to cool. Break into brittles. Alternatively mould candy into tiny cones while still warm and allow to cool.

KANTU

INGREDIENTS	Imperial	Metric	American
Sesame seeds, blanched	1 lb	450 g	1 lb
Water	4 fl. oz	100 ml	½ cup
Sugar	4 oz	100 g	½ cup
Lime or lemon juice	1 tsp	1 tsp	1 tsp

Soak and wash sesame by rubbing between the palms, changing the water until sesame is washed clean. Drain and dry on a flat surface. Bring sugar and water to the boil gradually, stirring constantly. Remove from the heat, add the lime juice and immediately stir in the sesame seeds. Mould into shapes by filling biscuit cutters with *kanto* on a board; allow to cool and harden. Store in a biscuit tin.

AVOCADO SPREAD

INGREDIENTS	Imperial	Metric	American
Medium avocado pear	1	1	1
Packet cracker biscuits	1	1	1

Even though the tree grows well in many parts of West Africa, the avocado tends to be regarded as foreign. It is usually eaten salted or spread on a hard biscuit called 'cabin biscuit'.

Peel and mash pear with a pinch of salt. Spread biscuit with a generous helping of mashed avocado. For special occasions, garnish the avocado biscuits with pieces of prawn, pineapple, cheese, etc.

NAKIA

INGREDIENTS	Imperial	Metric	American
Brown rice	1 lb	450 g	2 cups
Sugar	4 oz	100 g	½ cup
Chilli powder	2 tsp	2 tsp	2 tsp
Mixed gourd, clove, ginger, peppercorns	2 tsp	2 tsp	2 tsp

Wash rice well and rinse. Drain and spread on a flat surface to dry thoroughly. Grind rice into slightly coarse flour. Mix with a little water to form granules, turn into a steamer and put on top of a cooking pot half filled with water. Cover the steamer and steam rice for 30 minutes stirring to respread rice 3 or 4 times.

Grind, or turn into a mortar, add the rest of the ingredients and pound well with a pestle until all mixture is well blended. Mould into oblongs and arrange in a dish.

EBEREBE

INGREDIENTS	Imperial	Metric	American
Long pieces cassava, 4—6 in./10—15 cm	4	4	4
Large coconut	1	1	1

Peel the cassava, wash and boil the cassava without salt until cooked but not overdone. Allow to cool, slice very thinly with a sharp knife or slicer. Arrange in a dish garnished with pieces of shelled coconuts.

Eberebe is a favourite of the Ibos in East and Midwestern Nigeria. It is usually bought ready-to-eat from market women and provides the whole family with a delicious snack before the main lunch is cooked.

GROUNDNUT BUTTY

INGREDIENTS	Imperial	Metric	American
Freshly baked bread rolls	6	6	6
Shelled roasted groundnuts	4 oz	100 g	1 cup

Crush three-quarters of the groundnuts coarsely. Grind the rest into purée. Mix both together with a dash of salt. Cut each roll in half and spread the groundnut butter on each half. Serve with chilled beer.

CASHEW BRITTLE

INGREDIENTS	Imperial	Metric	American
Salted roasted cashew nuts	1 lb	450 g	1 lb
Sugar	4 oz	100 g	½ cup
Corn syrup	2 oz	50 g	⅛ cup + 1 tbsp
Lime or lemon juice	1½ tbsp	1½ tbsp	1½ tbsp
Pinch of salt			

Combine sugar, corn syrup and half cup of water in a saucepan and gradually bring to the boil, stirring constantly. Remove from heat and quickly stir in the butter and the lime juice. Allow to cool slightly and then stir in the cashew nuts. Pour mixture into a greased sandwich or shallow pan and allow to harden. Break into pieces and store.

RECIPE COMBINATIONS

RECIPE COMBINATIONS (cont.)

RECIPE COMBINATIONS (cont.)

INDEX

INDEX (cont.)

INDEX (cont.)

INDEX (cont.)